THE HARM DONE BY RELIGION

Edited by Ronald A. Lindsay,
Andrea Szalanski,
Nicole Scott, and Tom Flynn

INQUIRY PRESS
Amherst, NY

THE HARM DONE BY RELIGION

ISBN-10: 1937998045
ISBN-13: 978-1-937998-04-2

Articles in this book first appeared in

Free Inquiry

the flagship magazine of the Council for Secular Humanism.

CONTENTS

THE HARM DONE BY RELIGION

INTRODUCTION

Tom Flynn

> The knowledge exists by which universal happiness can be se-
> cured; the chief obstacle to its utilization for that purpose is the
> teaching of religion. Religion prevents our children from hav-
> ing a rational education; religion prevents us from removing the
> fundamental causes of war; religion prevents us from teaching
> the ethic of scientific co-operation in place of the old fierce doc-
> trines of sin and punishment. It is possible that mankind is on the
> threshold of a golden age; but if so, it will be necessary first to
> slay the dragon that guards the door, and that dragon is religion.
>
> —Bertrand Russell, "Has Religion Made
> Useful Contributions to Civilization?" (1930)

As a secular humanist activist who is outspokenly critical of religion, I am often faced with questions like this one: "Even if you're
right that there is no God and all religions are false, why be so
harsh about it? Religions have brought great beauty into the world,
and even if their doctrines are false many people draw comfort
from them. Why not adopt a more 'live and let live' approach?
After all, once you balance its positives against its negatives, what
harm has religion done?"

It's a fair question. Many answers are possible; some are collected in this anthology. Gregory Paul, an independent scholar
who penned one of the lengthiest and most excoriating historical

7

essays that *Free Inquiry* has published, might reply by pointing out that Adolf Hitler (building on a model developed by Benito Mussolini just a few years earlier) channeled massive state funding to Germany's Lutheran and Catholic churches. By doing so Hitler ensured that those powerful institutions would remain largely silent as Hitler's Nazi Party took power, tumbling Germany into genocidal madness and making a charnel house of Europe and much of the rest of the world. When the smoke cleared, the churches, the Vatican especially, continued to profit by Hitler's funding scheme—the only significant Nazi initiative that postwar Germany never rescinded—hugely enhancing the Catholic Church's strength and assuring its capacity to resist progressive reforms across the world right up to the present day.

I can't help thinking that it's going to take an awful lot of gorgeous cathedrals, devotional paintings, and Bach Masses to make up for that one.

The Harm Done by Religion is the third in a projected six-volume collection of outstanding articles published in *Free Inquiry* during roughly the first decade of my editorship, which began with the Winter 2000-01 issue. (Originally a quarterly, FI became a bimonthly publication with the October/November 2003 issue, which coincidentally contained the first installment of Gregory Paul's piece on religion's role in the rise of the Nazis.) This volume brings together classic essays from that period focusing on the fair and enduring question: "Why condemn religion? What harm has it done?" The snap answer is, religion has done terrible harm, and it's still doing it today.

What harm has religion done? Controversial ethicist (and for many years a *Free Inquiry* columnist) Peter Singer offers a searing case history of the George W. Bush Administration's 2001 decision to prohibit federal funding for most research involving human stem cells. That policy was inexplicable except in light of a certain strand of theology popular among American fundamentalist Evangelicals, and it hobbled an important sector of biomedical research. The damage it wreaked continues even today. Fourteen years later, what medical advances is humanity doing without because of this ham-handed and religion-inspired policy? The question is unanswerable. On a smaller scale, it resembles the unanswerable question of how much further advanced science, medicine, and the humanities might be today if the Roman church had not capitalized on the power vacuum resulting from the fall of Rome to drag the West into the Dark Ages.

Lisa Bauer was a shy American student when she converted to what seemed a fairly moderate strain of Islam here in the United States. Hers is not a story of radicalization and *jihadi* misadventure, but the experience was nonetheless deeply traumatic for her. That trauma was rooted in the structural misogyny that is inseparable from Islam even as it is practiced in the most politically temperate of mosques, and in the callousness of a local *imam* who facilitated her conversion but then pulled her into a tawdry life of sexual abuse that she endured for many years. Bauer chronicled her experiences in a searing 19,300-word memoir that appeared in three successive issues of FI in 2009 and 2010. It is bar none the lengthiest composition FI has published. Fortunately, it has a relatively happy ending: even while clinging to her damaging life as a *Muslimah,* Bauer was able to engage in solitary online research that eventually convinced her that the faith of Muhammad was untrue. Along the way, she reached out to Richard Dawkins (then a *Free Inquiry* columnist). She found employment by him as a webmaster and later as a senior researcher on one of his best-selling science books. At last she had landed in a place where she could start trying to repair the damage that her sojourn in Islam had visited upon her. Dawkins himself provides the introduction to Bauer's story; it is also included in this volume.

The indefatigable Christopher Hitchens (likewise, until his untimely death, an FI columnist) here offers two trenchant essays. One asks whether religion is a force for safety—or for greater danger—in each of a laundry-list of world trouble spots. Hitchens concludes that in Belfast, Beirut, and many other locales (he never gets past the Bs, but you get the idea) he would be far safer in a dark alley if a stranger approaching him were irreligious than if that stranger were a zealous adherent of whichever militant religious creed was locally dominant. (This example later appeared in his landmark book *god Is Not Great*.) His other essay chides the growing tendency to honor the holidays of a great parade of world religions on the calendars of large U.S. public school systems. America has welcomed adherents of almost every faith on earth; if we treat them all as expansively as supposedly-secular public schools treat, say, Christmas and the key Jewish holidays, will any time be left for instruction? And would some religious leaders actually be happier if there were none?

American readers who are not longtime freethinkers might not recognize the name of Barbara Smoker. That's too bad, because Smoker is a towering figure among atheists and humanists in the United Kingdom. Think of her as Britain's Madalyn Murray O'Hair, except that Smoker was a far more capable organizer. In addition she has enjoyed a productive, decades-long retirement in which she has continued playing the gadfly and making badly needed statements that others dared not. She appears in this volume with a searing rejection of the notion that Christianity, Islam, or any other faith should be able to claim immunity from criticism and satire. If anything, this 2006 essay is more relevant than ever today, when Muslim nations are outlawing criticism of religion (the United Arab Emirates), wheedling for all nations worldwide do likewise (Saudi Arabia), looking the other way as atheist bloggers are cut down by assassins on the streets (Bangladesh), or sentencing a freethought blogger to an inconceivable 1,000 lashes (Saudi Arabia again).

What question were we considering? Oh yes, what harm does religion do?

It would hardly be fair to compile an anthology like this one without including a couple of essays that skewer America's homegrown variations on the dark buffoonery of faith. FI Senior Editor James A. Haught contemplates the astonishing wealth that leading Christian televangelists have amassed—fortunes built largely on the small contributions of poor, often socially isolated TV viewers (the "widow's mite" indeed). And comedienne Beth Birnbaum chronicles a visit to a tacky Jesus park that still exists a few miles down the road from Disney World. It would all be laughable (and Birnbaum's narrative is infectiously hilarious) except for the dark agenda: Orlando's "Holy Land" park is really a thinly-disguised effort to ensnare Jews and convert them to Christianity.

Finally, a disturbing 2010 essay by writer Kristi DeMeester chronicles the lifelong damage that she suffered growing up in an obscure, highly insular Christian community that proscribed such worldly distractions as television and computers. It's tough to make your way in the workplace when you graduate from your faith school and you're one of the only job candidates who, handed a laptop, hasn't the faintest idea how to turn it on. Here we see yet another category of harm done by religion—less broadly destructive than Hitler's neutering of German churches but nonetheless devastating to those it afflicts.

What harm has religion done? I will close with an example from my own life. I grew up a deeply committed Roman Catholic. I believed it all. In my early adolescence I took a dark, calm delight in contemplating the "fact" that I had been so lucky as to be born into the one true faith and that all the Protestant and Jewish children I knew were going to hell. (I suppose I need hardly add that, born in 1955, I passed my childhood in the reactionary Catholic Church as it existed before the Second Vatican Council of the 1960s.) It didn't feel perverse to me then, though it surely does now.

Fortunately I never became the target of a pederast priest, but a more uneventful Catholic upbringing would expose me to trauma enough. It took me seven years of tortured, solitary, often furtive reading and research (starting at about age fourteen) to recognize first that Catholicism was untrue, secondly that Christianity was utterly false, and finally that even God did not exist. (Ironically, it was only at the conclusion of that intellectual odyssey that I discovered the literature of freethought, atheism, and humanism. How much faster and less painful my journey might have been if in those days that literature had been easier for a young person to discover!) For me, losing my religion was like withdrawal from some powerful drug. "Knowing" that I would live eternally, that I had an indispensable role to play in a cosmic drama that spanned the eons, that the very architect of the universe knew me, and had formed me, and loved me—these falsehoods were incalculably important to me. They were central to my identity not only as a Catholic but as a person; growing up, I had leaned on them extravagantly as I worked to craft the individual I would become. Realizing that they were all crude fictions was devastating. Realizing that my community, and even those closest to me, had worked relentlessly to addict me to this vast fabric of lies was more devastating still.

I suppose I should have known that I would lose the faith; the clues were there early enough. When I was in elementary school (rabid Catholic that I was, I nonetheless attended public schools; it's a long story) most of my classmates were Protestant. This was before the U.S. Supreme Court decisions of 1962 and 1963 barred officially-led prayers and Bible readings in public schools, and the public schools of Erie, Pennsylvania, engaged enthusiastically in both. I wasn't just a Catholic, I was as *deeply serious* a member of the pre-Vatican II church as a six-to-eight-year-old could be. So I knew that the version of the Lord's Prayer recited by a teacher each morning was the Protestant version (it had the closing stanza beginning "For thine is the kingdom and the glory and the power" which Catholicism rejected). I knew that the Bible from which the principal read over the school's public-address system each morning was the King James Bible, not the Douay-Rheims version which was the only Bible acceptable for Catholic devotion. I knew that my Catholic church was right. I knew that the Protestant churches were wrong—moreover, even when my age was in the single digits, I knew *in just what unique way* each principal Protestant denomination was wrong. (Chalk up half of that to my being a precocious child; chalk up the other half to the nuns in Catholic Sunday school, who imparted astonishing amounts of misinformation to their pupils in the limited time at their disposal.) The conclusion was inescapable: my community, my very *school* were busily engaged in purposely staining my soul with Protestant heresy. For whatever unaccountable reason, they wanted to endanger my salvation. They meant to do it; they schemed at it. I used to walk home from school (kids did in those days, and as a matter of fact it *was* uphill both ways), and each day I would do so terrified that a truck might jump the curb and snuff out my young life while my soul was in no condition to enter heaven.

I may have been the only Catholic eight-year-old who was silently cheering for Madalyn Murray O'Hair when in response to her case and one other the Supreme Court finally closed down the circus of Protestant indoctrination that had marred public education in Pennsylvania—indeed, in most Northeastern states—in the early 1960s. Perhaps even then I should have known that my Catholic commitment was too fevered, too brittle, to endure too much longer. But I didn't—I believed uncritically for another six years before I began my labored and harrowing crawl out from under the complex tissue of untruths that had been my faith.

There was one upside: My youthful experience as a Catholic recoiling from Protestant prayers gave me a visceral understanding of what it meant to be oppressed by imposition of a majority creed. After that preparation, understanding the issues surrounding the separation of church and state—and getting almost instantly passionate about them—were effortless for me.

What is the harm done by religion? It is as manifest as it is manifold, as you may better appreciate after reading the essays in this volume. I am not quite as optimistic as Bertrand Russell in 1930; I am less convinced than he was then that humankind stands at the threshold of a golden age. If we do, then I agree with him that the guardian blocking the door to tomorrow is religion, a dragon that should be slain or, if that is impossible, at least defanged, declawed, and shorn of its capacity to vomit fire. Then again, it may be more accurate to say that humanity stands not at the brink of a golden age, but rather in the shadow of terrifying existential threats: maybe the self-inflicted destruction of our fragile ecosphere, perhaps a literally world-shattering collision with a giant asteroid. Even if that is the case—even if humanity's highest challenge is merely to overcome an apocalyptic peril in hopes of living to muddle through another day—the dragon of religion will richly deserve our most vigorous efforts to vanquish it.

Imagine a scenario of searing irony. Imagine that ten years from now we discover a world-killer space rock headed straight for Earth. The planet's greatest scientists and engineers and thinkers and business leaders feverishly confer. Heads downcast, they emerge from their council chamber and announce that the asteroid cannot be deflected. If only our technology had been fifty years more advanced, they say dejectedly, we would stand a good chance of turning it away.

What harm will we "credit" to the Dark Ages then?

I rest my case.

Tom Flynn is the editor of Free Inquiry, *the executive director of the Council for Secular Humanism, and editor of* The New Encyclopedia of Unbelief *(2007).*

Touring Orlando's 'Holy Land'

Monday in the Theme Park with Jesus

Beth Birnbaum

In the year of their Lord 2001, on February 5, drought-fueled brush fires burned outside my Orlando hotel-room window: real fires, not the burning bush or even George W. Bush allusions. As everyone else prayed for rain, the prayers of Zion's Hope, doing business as "The Holy Land Experience," were answered with a sunny, arid, picture-perfect, grand-opening day.

When I arrived, the huge protest promised by Jewish Defense League (JDL) Chairman Irv Rubin—ballyhooed by Cable News Network, the *New York Times*, the Orlando press, and even the British Broadcasting Company—consisted of Mr. Rubin and another JDL member holding either end of a banner. Mr. Rubin, in from Los Angeles for the event, invited me to join him and his friend in demanding a warning label identifying the theme park as Christian. Nearby, a man on a white horse (unaffiliated with Mr. Rubin) was explaining to eighteen reporters that he had been sent by the Lord to love everyone.

Orlando rabbis, avoiding association with the militant JDL— or the chance of giving the theme park free publicity—reserved the right to protest at a later date. Christian groups also criticized the park as trivializing religion.

An Experience official charitably handed me a two-dollar discount off the seventeen-dollar (children under Bar Mitzvah age, twelve dollars) cover price. As I followed the path to Theme Park Jerusalem, gray concrete gave way to a red faux-dirt road complete with cracks, donkey-shoe imprints, and camel-hoof tracks. Cecil B. DeMillesque Roman music blared forth. The non-Kosher Oasis Palms Café (Bedouin Beef Wraps: just $6.95) played Arabic music. Jewish areas featured a violin-laden rip-off of the *Schindler's List* soundtrack, and the Christian areas broadcast a heavenly chorus of twenty voices complete with harps.

I was pleased to see signs proclaiming "The Holy Land Experience is a nonsmoking facility," wheelchair friendly, and forbids lewd and lascivious behavior and unauthorized religious activity.

After a girl clothed in ancient garb of polyester blend slipped a ticket through the bulletproof window, I entered the gates. The walls, expensively "weathered" with pride by skilled scenic artisans, rivaled the fireplace mantle I once marbleized using a kit. In New York, we could have rendered it ancient in weeks for free, sidewalk gum spots optional.

A teenage girl authentically costumed but for blue designer braces shrilly called for all to come to the Marketplace, where everything was 50 percent off. This proved untrue, but the refreshment stands did sell milk and honey ice cream at a reasonable two dollars and fifty cents a cup. The gift shops lulled Jews into a false sense of security, and allowed Christians the chance to play archeologist, by carrying Jewish merchandise: menorahs, prayer shawls, books, Holy Land Experience logo apparel, and decorative objects including an eight-hundred-dollar silver-plated Moses. There were no golden calves.

There was an also extensive line of books and tapes by Baptist minister Marv Rosenthal, *née* New Jersey Jew and the force behind the sixteen-million-dollar "Holy Land Experience." One item, a four-dollar-and-ninety-nine-cent pamphlet, takes Jews step by step through conversion to Christianity.

A Gen-Xer checked out *The Fourth Reich* by Robert Van Kampen, a thriller about cloning Hitler that was considered science fiction before Dolly the sheep. "What's the Fourth Reik?" she asked. Her boyfriend replied it was the Nazis. (They were into biblical stuff, but not up to speed on the twentieth century.)

Reporters, cameramen, and sound crews were everywhere, including CNN's Alexa Lee in a black suit, standing in the hot sun and interviewing herself. When a reporter asked my opinion, I gushed that the Holy Land Experience was just like the Caesar's Palace Mall in Vegas, but with a real sky. Maybe they'll put a casino in the Temple and let Jesus close it down.

I missed most of the pageant that took place on the steps of "The Plaza of The Nations," but arrived in time to see that their Madonna wears a microphone hooked around her head just like the pop star. Wandering around the five developed acres of the park, I came across "Calvary's Garden Tomb." An opening "carved" in the concrete rocks contained a lantern, a shelf holding a rumpled sheet, and a sign proclaiming, "He is not here for He has risen." Nearby were the as-yet-unopened "Qumran Dead Sea Caves," slated to hold real biblical artifacts. According to the brochure, they're made of steel tubing and 165,000 pounds of hand-carved concrete (82.5 tons isn't as impressive). At The Plaza of the Nations, located in front of "The Palace of the Great King," a group of five men (one Black, one Asian, three White) and four White women were singing peppy, quasi-rock, Gospel-free versions of "Give Me that Old Time Religion" and other pro-Jesus tunes. A few people were smiling and clapping, but most were looking for room on the benches. The lack of seating while viewing or waiting for attractions was a major complaint. Except for three Koreans, one African-American woman, and a few families with children, the crowd was made up mostly of gray-haired White people.

Waiting on line at "The Wilderness Tabernacle," we were entertained by a costumed Shofar-blowing actor/theme park character. He complained that the Shofar, a carved ram's horn trumpet used to call for worship or battle, stunk like a dead animal. (They're available in the gift shop, in seventy-five and one-hundred-and-twenty-five-dollar sizes.)

Inside the black-walled theater, the stage setting befitted a minimalist avant-garde postmodern way way off-Broadway production. There was a twenty-five-foot-long, fifteen-foot-wide piece of fabric slung across the stage with Ultrasuede "animal" skins hanging at the top. A small wooden deck held a special effects barbecue for burnt offerings. A five-foot-square black *schmatta* (rag) hung from the ceiling on which to project images.

The guy from outside welcomed us as Moses's brother Aaron. After a recorded cantor sang Jewish prayers, a Borg (as in *Star Trek*)-like chorus narrated the story of the Tabernacle after the Ten Commandments. They avoided chanting, "You will be assimilated" or "Resistance is futile."

After smoke and light rituals around the "barbecue," we were treated to Indiana Jones-type special effects when the Ark of the Covenant blasted carbon dioxide and water/glycol-based "fog juice" into the air at forty miles an hour. At the end, the voices chanted that one day the promise of Zion would be fulfilled. A white outline of Mary and Joseph holding the baby Jesus momentarily flashed on the *schmatta* to deliver an almost subliminal message. This is just part of the reason that Jewish groups are so negative about the Holy Land Experience. Still, it took me three days to figure out that "Zion's Hope" meant Jesus; the last two thousand years of history prevented me from easily leaping to that conclusion.

Next, I wandered into a building containing the world's largest indoor model of Jerusalem (about twenty-by-thirty feet), billed as such because there's a larger one outdoors in the real Jerusalem. This, the Mother of All Dioramas, was built to show Jerusalem in 66 C.E., including the hills, roads, homes, temples, and teeny-tiny people. The walls were made out of giant wooden Lego-type blocks, spray painted with stucco finish. I was disappointed there were no electric trains.

Waiting on line to see the movie *The Seed of Promise* at the Theater of Life, I met the filmmaker: Keith Kolbo of ITCF Entertainment, a company famous for theme-park development. Kolbo gleefully related how "God provided" newly unemployed construction workers from the just-completed Universal Theme Park City Walk to build the Holy Land. (Note: ITCF also built Bob Marley Land, where, despite its "holy" significance, Ganja is forbidden.) God also provided funding; the developers profitably sold six acres of land to the government for an Interstate 4 off-ramp.

The movie began. Jesus's arm was being nailed to the cross, blood running from His wound. Next, there were dizzying blurred action images of the Romans approaching the Temple with a battering ram, fleeing townspeople, and flashes of the Jewish priests inside preparing a sacrificial lamb. The battering of the door was interspersed (in all its New York University second-year film school student glory) with the hammering of the nails into Jesus, creating a macabre anvil chorus. The only things missing were the A-bomb mushroom cloud, the Hindenburg explosion, and Eisenstein's scene of the baby carriage careening down the Odessa Steps.

The movie segued into computer-generated Creation (no evolution here). The tastefully shown naked edges of Adam and Eve in Paradise became terrified, fig-leafed people, fighting for modesty as they fled a wrathful God, His wrathful storm, and the evil slithery snake. Between more cuts of the Romans attacking the Temple and nailing Jesus, Abraham tearfully bound his son's hands to sacrifice him according to the Lord's wishes. As he reached up to plunge the knife into his son, it was flung from his hand by a heavenly *Star Wars* light-saber effect accompanied by the Voice of God. The circumcision that took place after this event was mercifully deleted. The narrator described Jesus's efforts curing the ill: the greater the sins, the sicker the sinner, the harder the healing. This undoubtedly cheered up the folks watching in wheelchairs.

Back to Jesus. As the hammering was completed, the scene shifted to the Temple door being rammed open and the Jewish priests fleeing. The lamb, grateful to be rescued from those nasty Jews by the Romans (at least it wasn't a Christian child being sacrificed: that would have started a pogrom), ran off and magically appeared on a grassy hill with blue sky and rolling clouds behind it.

Flash to two sad guys walking down the road. The camera faced them from the perspective of a traveler. It turned out he's Jesus, newly risen from the dead, who reassured them He's O.K. and led them to a conveniently located wooden picnic table for lunch. I expected Yogi and Boo Boo in a cameo.

Next Jesus (shown from the back) replaced the lamb on the grassy hill. Men, women, and children from all walks of life and many lands—an international "Village People"—walked towards Him wearing glassy stares and beatific smiles. Jesus greeted them like a rock star on his way to the stage. My feet suddenly became cold and clammy, and it wasn't chills running down my spine. I looked down to discover dry ice smoke rolling across the floor to simulate clouds and make us part of the movie action. I fled before frostbite could set in.

One of the goals of The Holy Land Experience, subtly (and not so subtly) stated, is the conversion of Jews to Christianity. Unlike Woody Allen, who marries *shiksas,* former Jew Marv Rosenthal deals with his Jewish identity and guilt problems by turning Christian, then pleading with Christians to forgive him for being "chosen," to accept Judaism as their own roots, and to see Jews as next in line for redemption. It's theological "I agree, don't hit me, you'll break my glasses." It all nicely dovetails with George W. Bush's view of America. A man who believes in the government funding of faith-based charity should love the idea of faith-based amusement parks. It also addresses what he considers to be the very real problem of unconverted Jews going to hell.

Even though it shares the same goal as the Spanish Inquisition, which was free, The Holy Land Experience accepts VISA, MasterCard, Amex, Discover, personal checks with proper iden-tification, and cash. (Naturally there are no ATMs.) It also is less stressful, and more user-friendly, and entertaining than the Inquisition ever was. All in all, it's the perfect Bush-era field trip for your local voucher/charter faith-based school.

Beth Birnbaum is a freelance writer and stand-up comedian in New York City.

ARE FAITH AND SAFETY INVERSELY RELATED?

Christopher Hitchens

A few days before the assault on American civil society by faith-based death squads, I was a member of a panel discussion at a conservative weekend conference. I gave it as my opinion that there was no means of deriving ethics from religion, and that a moral life was not only possible without supernatural support, but in fact more feasible. I was challenged by Dennis Prager, the right-wing media performer. He insisted that he could accept my view only on condition that I gave a "yes or no" answer to the following question: "Suppose you are lost in a strange town and it is late at night. You see a group of men coming toward you. Do you feel more safe, or less safe, on learning that they have just come from a prayer meeting?"

I like to think that I can "do" fast-service panel or chat-show questions without rehearsal, but I have to admit that I was momentarily unhorsed by the sheer fatuity of this. (For one thing, as phrased, it wasn't a "yes-no" question. It was an "either-or" question.) Further, while Mr. Prager clearly regarded it as a trick question, I have—unlike him—been in exactly that hypothetical position several times. Without leaving the letter *B* in the alphabet, I can say that in Belfast, Beirut, and Belgrade I have been on the

25

streets at odd hours and been compelled to wonder about exactly who is coming toward me. In each case, if I were the praying type, I would have been fervently beseeching that the men had *not* just wound up a session at the Martyr's Memorial Church, or the Party of God local, or the Serbian Orthodox hangout. But who, in the context, could I have been beseeching?

The absurdity of this dilemma is well known to anyone who has ever been, even for an intellectual instant, an atheist in a foxhole. It is precisely at such moments that the emptiness of revealed religion becomes much more, rather than less, evident. Which is why it is so depressing to see even the most vivid such moments conscripted by the unscrupulous peddlers of revelation. After all, easily the most devout people on the four civilian aircraft of September 11 were the men who murdered their passengers and many others and killed themselves in the process. But not even this random encounter with the devout, which took place in broad daylight, has been enough to put a dent in the fallacy.

Everybody remembers the frightful remarks made by Jerry Falwell and Pat Robertson in the immediate aftermath of the September aggression. They said openly that the attacks were a punishment for a society wedded to materialism and sexual pluralism, and were duly ridiculed for it. But only a few days later, at a solemn memorial service at the National Cathedral, Billy Graham told the assembled American establishment that the murder victims were all safe and happy in paradise. He added that they would not wish to return even if they could. This insult to the grieving relatives, delivered while the ruins were still smoldering, was also an insult to the intelligence of a whole society. Yet nobody saw fit to point out that this view had received, so to speak, official endorsement. (Always an honored guest at the White House, Graham soon afterwards received a knighthood from Her Majesty Queen Elizabeth.) His son and successor got into some mild hot water for saying that Islam was essentially a wicked religion, but again nobody was on hand to point out that, in the matter of knowing all about the sumptuous character of Paradise and how to get there, the Grahams and the Al Qaeda forces were reading from the same page.

In succeeding weeks, the Greek Orthodox patriarch in Athens unburdened himself of the view that the attacks were a divine judgment on America, and a group of Christians and Jews convened by Rabbi Daniel Lapine vented the same thought in a prominent advertisement on the op-ed page of the *New York Times*. So in a bizarre form of reverse ecumenism, prominent spokesmen for all branches of religion have in one way or another endorsed Osama bin Laden's statement that the United States is "the world leader of atheism." If only this were true. Instead, even in a country that is in many ways the world capital of materialism, people voluntarily disarm themselves by the belief that, if a group is coming toward them with religious intent, that intent must somehow be benign.

*　*　*

You often hear that the Catholic Church has become more tolerant and "inclusive." You also often hear that, at any rate, it instructs its members in logic (if not in reason). I had personal experience to the contrary on a recent book-tour stop in San Francisco. Michael Krasny, the popular and literate host of *Forum* on KQED, had invited me to be his guest. He received an e-mail from Maurice Healy of the Catholic Archdiocese, asking him to cancel my appearance. The reason given was an interview I had conducted with *Free Inquiry*, in which I repeated my atheist views. Mr. Krasny read the e-mail on the air and also replied to it in person, saying that his show did not discriminate against unbelievers. I later wrote to Healy, asking if he spoke for himself or for his bishop. He responded in hurt tones, saying that he did not want to censor anyone, let alone discriminate, but that some views, such as those in *Free Inquiry*, were just too much to take.

I find this instructive, as well as amusing, for three reasons. First, it shows that the term *infidel* means to some Catholics exactly what it means to some extremist Muslims. Second, it shows that some people (this man identified himself as "director of Communications and Outreach"!) cannot make the elementary distinction between abhorring a view and seeking to censor it. Third, it shows that *Free Inquiry* is read in all the right places.

Christopher Hitchens is a columnist for Vanity Fair *and the* Nation *and the author most recently of* Unacknowledged Legislation: Writers in the Public Sphere.

THE GREAT SCANDAL
PART 1
CHRISTIANITY'S ROLE IN THE RISE OF THE NAZIS

Gregory S. Paul

You know what happens when atheists take over—remember Nazi Germany?" Many Christians point to Nazism, alongside Stalinism, to illustrate the perils of atheism in power.[1] At the other extreme, some authors paint the Vatican as Hitler's eager ally. Meanwhile, the Nazis are generally portrayed as using terror to bend a modern civilization to their agenda; yet we recognize that Hitler was initially popular. Amid these contradictions, where is the truth?

A growing body of scholarly research, some based on careful analysis of Nazi records, is clarifying this complex history.[2] It reveals a convoluted pattern of religious and moral failure in which atheism and the nonreligious played little role, except as victims of the Nazis and their allies. In contrast, Christianity had the capacity to stop Nazism before it came to power, and to reduce or moderate its practices afterwards, but repeatedly failed to do so because the principal churches were complicit with—indeed, in the pay of—the Nazis.

Most German Christians supported the Reich; many continued to do so in the face of mounting evidence that the dictatorship was depraved and murderously cruel. Elsewhere in Europe the story was often the same. Only with Christianity's forbearance and fre-

29

quent cooperation could fascistic movements gain majority support in Christian nations. European fascism was the fruit of a Christian culture. Millions of Christians actively supported these notorious regimes. Thousands participated in their atrocities.

What, in God's name, were they thinking?

Before we can consider the Nazis, we need to examine the historical and cultural religious context that would give rise to them.

CHRISTIAN FOUNDATIONS

Early Christian sects promoted loyalty to authoritarian rulers so long they were not intolerably anti-Christian or, worse, atheistic. Christian anti-Semitism sprang from one of the church's first efforts to forge an accommodation with power. Reinterpreting the Gospels to shift blame for the Crucifixion from the Romans to the Jews (the "Christ killer" story) courted favor with Rome, an early example of Christian complicity for political purposes. Added energy came from Christians' anger over most Jews' refusal to convert.[3]

Christian anti-Semitism was only intermittently violent, but when violence occurred it was devastating. The first outright extermination of Jews occurred in 414 C.E. It would have innumerable successors, the worst nearly genocidal in scope. At standard rates of population growth, Diaspora Jewry should now number in the hundreds of millions. That there are only an estimated 13 million Jews in the world[4] is largely the result of Christian violence and forced conversion.[5]

Anti-Semitic practices pioneered by Catholics included the forced wearing of yellow identification, ghettoization, confiscation of Jews' property, and bans on intermarriage with Christians. European Protestantism bore the fierce impress of Martin Luther, whose 1543 tract *On the Jews and Their Lies* was a principal inspiration for *Mein Kampf*.[6] In addition to his anti-Semitism, Luther was also a fervent authoritarian. *Against the Robbing and Murdering Peasants*, his vituperative commentary on a contemporary rebellion, contributed to the deaths of perhaps 100,000 Christians and helped to lay the groundwork for an increasingly severe Germo-Christian autocracy.[7]

With the Enlightenment, deistic and secular thinkers seeded Western culture with Greco-Roman notions of democracy and free expression. The feudal aristocracies and the churches counterattacked, couching their reactionary defense of privilege in self-consciously biblical language. This controversy would shape centuries of European history. As late as 1870, the Roman Catholic Church reaffirmed a reactionary program at the first Vatican Council. Convened by the ultraconservative Pope Pius IX (reigned 1846–1878), Vatican I stridently condemned modernism, democracy, capitalism, usury, and Marxism.[8] Anti-Semitism was also part of the mix; well into the twentieth century, mainstream Catholic publications set an intolerant tone that later Nazi propaganda would imitate. Anti-Semitism remained conspicuous in mainstream Catholic literature even after Pope Pius XI (reigned 1922–1939) officially condemned it.

Protestantism, too, was largely hostile toward modernism and democracy during this period (with a few exceptions in northern Europe). Because Jews were seen as materialists who promoted and benefited from Enlightenment modernism, most Protestant denominations remained anti-Semitic.

With the nineteenth century came a European movement that viewed Judaism as a racial curse. Attracting both Protestant and Catholic dissidents within Germanic populations, Aryan Christianity differed from traditional Christianity in denying both that Christ was a Jew and that Christianity had grown out of Judaism.[9] Adherents viewed Christ as a divine Aryan warrior who brought the sword to cleanse the earth of Jews.[10] Aryans were held to be the only true humans, specially created by God through Adam and Eve; all other peoples were soulless subhumans, descended from apes or created by Satan with no hope of salvation.[11] Most non-Aryans were considered suitable for subservient roles including slavery, but not the Jews. Spiritless yet clever and devious, Jews were seen as a satanic disease to be quarantined or eliminated.

During the same years neopagan and occult movements gained adherents and incubated their own form of Aryanism. Unlike Aryan Christians, neopagan Aryans acknowledged that Christ was a Jew—and for that reason rejected Christianity. They believed themselves descended from demigods whose divinity had degraded through centuries of interbreeding with lesser races. The Norse gods and even the Atlantis myth sometimes decorated Aryan mythology.

Attempting to deny that Nazi anti-Semitism had a Christian component, Christian apologists exaggerate the influence of Aryan neopaganism. Actually, neopaganism never had a large following.

German Aryanism, whether Christian or pagan, became known as "Volkism." Volkism prophesied the emergence of a great God-chosen Aryan who would lead the people (*Volk*) to their grand destiny through the conquest of *Lebensraum* (living space). A common motto was "God and *Volk*." Disregarding obvious theological contradictions, growing numbers of German nationalists managed to work Aryanism into their Protestant or Catholic confessions, much as contemporary adherents of *Voudoun* or *Santería* blend the occult with their Christian beliefs. Darwinian theory sometimes entered Volkism as a belief in the divinely intended survival of the fittest peoples. Democracy had no place, but Nietzschean philosophy had some influence—a point Christian apologists make much of. Yet Nietzsche's influence was modest, as Volkists found his skepticism toward religion unacceptable.[12]

Though traceable to the ancient world, atheism first emerged as a major social movement in the mid-1800s.[13] It would be associated with both pro- and antidemocratic worldviews. Strongly influenced by science, atheists tended to view all humans as descended in common from apes. There was no inherent anti-Semitic tradition. Some atheists accepted then-popular pseudoscientific racist views that the races exhibited varying levels of intellect due to differing genetic heritages. Some went further, embracing various forms of eugenics as a means of improving the human condition. But neither of these positions was uniquely or characteristically atheistic. "Scientific" racism is actually better understood as a tool by which Christians could perpetuate their own cultural prejudices—it was no accident that the races deemed inferior by Western Christian societies and "science" were the same!

When we seek precursors of Nazi anti-Semitism and authoritarianism, it is among European Christians, not among the atheists, that we must search.

Following World War I, the religious situation in Europe was complex. Scientific findings about the age of the Earth, Darwin's theory of evolution, and biblical criticism had fueled the first major expansion of nontheism at Christianity's expense among ordinary Europeans. The churches' support for the catastrophic Great War further fueled public disaffection, as did (in Germany) the flight of the Kaiser, in whom both Protestant and Catholic clergy had invested heavily.[14] But religion was not everywhere in retreat: postwar Germany experienced a Christian spiritual renaissance outside the traditional churches.[15] Religious freedom was unprecedented, but the established churches enjoyed widespread state support and controlled their own education systems. They were far more influential than today.

Roughly two-thirds of Germans were Protestant, almost all of the rest Catholic. The pagan minority claimed at most 5 percent. Explicit nontheism was limited to an intellectual elite and to committed socialists. Just 1.5 percent of Germans identified themselves as unbelievers in a 1939 census, which means either that very few Nazis and National Socialist German Worker's Party supporters were atheists, or that atheists feared to identify themselves to the pro-theistic regime.

Most religious Germans detested the impiety, secularism, and hedonistic decadence that they associated with such modernist ideas as democracy and free speech. If they feared democracy, they were terrified by Communism, to the point of being willing to accept extreme countermethods.

Thus it was a largely Christian, deeply racist, often antidemocratic, and in many respects dangerously primitive Western culture into which Nazism would arise. It was a theistic powder keg ready to explode.

"Thou shalt smite them, and utterly destroy them, thou shalt make no covenant with them, nor show mercy unto them. And thou shalt consume all the people which the Lord thy God shall deliver thee; thine eye shall have no pity upon them. . . . For they will turn away thy son from following me . . . so will the anger of the Lord be kindled against you, and destroy thee suddenly . . . the Lord thy God hath chosen thee to be a special people unto himself, above all people that are on the face of the earth."

— *Deuteronomy 7:3–6, God's orders to the Israelites on how to conquer and cleanse all of Canaan*

"But since I learned that these miserable and accursed people to lure themselves even to us. . . . I have published this little book. . . .Our Lord calls them a "brood of vipers.". . . Therefore the blind Jews are truly stupid fools . . . wherever they have their synagogues, nothing is found but a den of devils in which sheer self-glory, conceit, lies, blasphemy, and defaming of God and men are practiced most maliciously . . . they are nothing but thieves and robbers who daily eat no morsel and wear no thread of clothing which they have not stolen and pilfered from us by means of their accursed usury. . . . Did I not tell you earlier that a Jew is such a noble, precious jewel that God and all the angels dance when he farts? . . . We must avoid confirming them in their wanton lying, slandering, cursing and defaming. Nor dare we make ourselves partners in their devilish ranting and raving by shielding and protecting them, by giving them food, drink and shelter, or by other neighborly acts . . . gentle mercy will only tend to make them worse and worse, while sharp mercy will reform them but little. Therefore, in any case, away with them! . . . their synagogues must be burned down . . . their prayer books, their Talmudic writings, also the entire Bible—be taken from them . . . they be forbidden . . . to pray, to teach publicly. . . . They must be driven from our country. . . . May Christ, our dear Lord, convert them mercifully and preserve us steadfastly and immovably in the knowledge of him, which is eternal life. Amen.

— *a sample from Luther's* On The Jews and Their Lies

NAZI LEADERS, THEISM, AND FAMILY VALUES

According to standard biographies, the principal Nazi leaders were all born, baptized, and raised Christian. Most grew up in strict, pious households where tolerance and democratic values were disparaged. Nazi leaders of Catholic background included Adolf Hitler, Heinrich Himmler, Reinhard Heydrich, and Joseph Goebbels.

Hitler did well in monastery school. He sang in the choir, found High Mass and other ceremonies intoxicating, and idolized priests. Impressed by their power, he at one time considered entering the priesthood.

Rudolf Hoess, who as commandant at Auschwitz-Birkinau pioneered the use of the Zyklon-B gas that killed half of all Holocaust victims, had strict Catholic parents. Hermann Goering had mixed Catholic-Protestant parentage, while Rudolf Hess, Martin Bormann, Albert Speer, and Adolf Eichmann had Protestant backgrounds. Not one of the top Nazi leaders was raised in a liberal or atheistic family—no doubt, the parents of any of them would have found such views scandalous. Traditionalists would never think to deprive their offspring of the faith-based moral foundations that they would need to grow into ethical adults.

So much for the Nazi leaders' religious backgrounds. Assessing their religious views as adults is more difficult. On ancillary issues such as religion, Party doctrine was a deliberate tangle of contradictions.[16] For Hitler, consistency mattered less than having a statement at hand for any situation that might arise. History records many things that Hitler wrote or said about religion, but they too are sometimes contradictory. Many were crafted for a particular audience or moment and have limited value for illuminating Hitler's true opinion; in any case, neither Hitler nor any other key Nazi leader was a trained theologian with carefully thought-out views.

Accuracy of transcription is another concern. Hitler's public speeches were recorded reliably, but were often propagandistic. His private statements seem more likely to reflect his actual views, but their reliability varies widely.[17] The passages Christian apologists cite most often to prove Hitler's atheism are of questionable accuracy. Apologists often brandish them without noting historians' reservations. Hitler's personal library has been partly preserved, and a good deal is known about his reading habits, another possible window onto Hitler's beliefs.[18] Also important, and often ignored by apologists, are statements made by religious figures of the time, who generally—at least for public consumption—viewed Hitler as a Christian and a Catholic in good standing. Meanwhile, the silent testimony of photographs is irrefutable, much as apologists struggle to evade this damning visual evidence.

Despite these difficulties, enough is known to build a reasonable picture of what Hitler and other top Nazis believed.

Hitler was a Christian, but his Christ was no Jew. In his youth he dabbled with occult thinking but never became a devotee. As a young man he grew increasingly bohemian and stopped attending church. Initially no more anti-Semitic than the norm, in the years before the Great War he fell under the anti-Semitic influence of the Volkish Christian Social Party and other Aryan movements. After Germany's stunning defeat and the ruinous terms of peace, Hitler became a full-blown Aryanist and anti-Semite. He grew obsessed with racial issues, which he unfailingly embedded in a religious context.

Apologists often suggest that Hitler did not hold a traditional belief in God because he believed that *he* was God. True, Hitler thought himself God's chosen leader for the Aryan race. But he never claimed to be divine, and never presented himself in that manner to his followers. Members of the *Wehrmacht* swore this loyalty oath: "I swear by God this holy oath to the Führer of the German Reich and the German people, Adolf Hitler." For Schutzstaffel (S.S.) members it was: "I pledge to you, Adolf Hitler, my obedience unto death, so help me God."

Hitler repeatedly thanked God or Providence for his survival on the western front during the Great War, his safe escape from multiple assassination attempts, his seemingly miraculous rise from homelessness to influence and power, and his amazing international successes. He never tired of proclaiming that all of this was beyond the power of any mere mortal. Later in the war, Hitler portrayed German defeats as part of an epic test: God would reward his true chosen people with the final victory they deserved so long as they never gave up the struggle.

Reich iconography, too, reveals that Nazism never cut its ties to Christianity. The markings of *Luftwaffe* aircraft comprised just two swastikas—and six crosses. Likewise the *Kreigsmarine* (German Navy) flag combined the symbols. Hitler participated in public prayers and religious services at which the swastika and the cross were displayed together.

Hitler openly admired Martin Luther, whom he considered a brilliant reformer.[19] Yet he said in several private conversations that he considered himself a Catholic. He said publicly on several occasions that Christ was his savior. As late as 1944, planning the last-ditch offensive the world would know as the Battle of the Bulge, he code-named it "Operation Christrose."

Among his Nazi cronies Hitler criticized the established churches harshly and often. Some of these alleged statements must be treated with skepticism,[20] but clearly he viewed the traditional Christian faiths as weak and contaminated by Judaism. Still, there is no warrant for the claim that he became anti-Christian or antireligious after coming to power. No reliably attributed quote reveals Hitler to be an atheist or in any way sympathetic to atheism. On the contrary, he often condemned atheism, as he did Christians who collaborated with such atheistic forces as Bolshevism. He consistently denied that the state could replace faith and instructed Speer to include churches in his beloved plans for a rebuilt Berlin. The Nazi-era constitution explicitly evoked God. Calculating that his victories over Europe and Bolshevism would make him so popular that people would be willing to abandon their traditional faiths, Hitler entertained plans to replace Protestantism and Catholicism with a reformed Christian church that would include all Aryans while removing foreign (Rome-based) influence. German Protestants had already rejected a more modest effort along these lines, as will be seen below. How Germans as a whole would have received this reform after a Nazi victory is open to question. In any case, Hitler saw himself as Christianity's ultimate reformer, not its dedicated enemy. Hitler was a complex figure, but based on the available evidence we can conclude our inquiry into his personal religious convictions by describing him as an Aryan Volkist Christian who had deep Catholic roots, strongly influenced by Protestantism, touched by strands of neopaganism and Darwinism, and minimally influenced by the occult. Though Hitler pontificated about God and religion at great length, he considered politics more important than religion as the means to achieve his agenda.

None of the leaders immediately beneath Hitler was a pious traditional Christian. But there is no compelling evidence that any top Nazi was nontheistic. Any so accused denied the charge with vehemence.

From *La Civilta Cattoloica* (primary Vatican publication):

"[The Jewish nation] does not work, but traffics in the property and the work of others, it does not produce, but lives and grows fat with the products of the arts and industry of the nations that give it refuge. It is the giant octopus that with its oversized tentacles envelops everything. It has its stomach in the banks . . . and its suction cups everywhere: in contracts and monopolies, in credit unions and banks, in shipping and in the railroads, in the town treasuries and in state finance. It represents the kingdom of capital . . . the aristocracy of gold. . . . It reigns unopposed." *(1893)*

"The world is sick. . . . Everywhere peoples are in the grip of inexplicable convulsions. Who is responsible? The Synagogue." *(1922)*

". . . an obvious fact that the Jews are a disruptive element because of their dominating spirit and their revolutionary tendency. Judaism is . . . a foreign body that irritates and provokes the reactions of the organism it has contaminated." *(1937)*

"While the regime is determined to carry through the political and moral purging of our public life, it is creating and ensuring the prerequisites for a really deep inner religiosity. Benefits of a personal nature, which might arise from a compromise with atheistic organizations, could outweigh the results which become apparent through the destruction of general religious-ethical values. The national regime seeks in both Christian confessions the factors most important for the maintenance of our Volkism. The struggle against a materialistic philosophy and for the creation of a true folk community serves the interests of the German nation as well as our Christian belief."

— Hitler, in his first speech to the Reichstag

Reich-Führer Himmler regularly attended Catholic services until he lurched into an increasingly bizarre Aryanism. He authorized searches for the Holy Grail and other supposedly powerful Christian and Cathar relics. A believer in reincarnation, he sent expeditions to Tibet and the American tropics in search of the original Aryans and even Atlantians. He and Heydrich modeled the S.S. after the disciplined and secretive Jesuits; it would not accept atheists as members.[21] Goering, least ideological among top Nazis, sometimes endorsed both Protestant and Catholic traditions. On other occasions he criticized them. Goebbels turned against Catholicism in favor of a reformed Aryan faith; both his and Goering's children were baptized. Bormann was stridently opposed to contemporary organized Christianity; he was a leader of the Church Struggle, the inconsistently applied Nazi campaign to oppose the influence of established churches.[22]

The Nazis championed traditional family values: their ideology was conservative, bourgeois, patriarchal, and strongly antifeminist. Discipline and conformity were emphasized, marriage promoted, abortion and homosexuality despised.[23]

Traditionalism also dominated Nazi philosophy, such as it

was. Though science and technology were lauded, the overall thrust opposed the Enlightenment, modernism, intellectualism, and rationality. It is hard to imagine how a movement with that agenda could have been friendly toward atheism, and the Nazis were not. Volkism was inherently hostile toward atheism: free-thinkers clashed frequently with Nazis in the late 1920s and early 1930s. On taking power, Hitler banned freethought organizations and launched an "anti-godless" movement. In a 1933 speech he declared: "We have . . . undertaken the fight against the atheistic movement, and that not merely with a few theoretical declarations: we have stamped it out." This forthright hostility was far more straightforward than the Nazis' complex, often contradictory stance toward traditional Christian faith.

DESTROYING DEMOCRACY: A POLITICAL-RELIGIOUS COLLABORATION

As detailed by historian Ian Kershaw, Hitler made no secret of his intent to destroy democracy. Yet he came to power largely legally; in no sense was he a tyrant imposed upon the German people.

The Nazi takeover climaxed a lengthy, ironic rejection of democracy *at the hands of a majority of German voters.* By the

"I am now as before a Catholic and will always remain so."

— *Statement by Hitler to General Gerhart Engel in 1941*

"I learned much from the Order of the Jesuits. Until now, there has never been anything more grandiose, on the earth, than the hierarchical organization of the Catholic church. I transferred much of this organization into my own party."

— *Hitler, 1933*

early 1930s, ordinary Germans had lost patience with democracy; growing numbers hoped an authoritarian strongman would restore order and prosperity and return Germany to great-power status. Roughly two-thirds of German Christians *repeatedly* voted for candidates who promised to overthrow democracy. Authoritarianism was all but inevitable; at issue was merely who the new strongman would be.

What made democracy so fragile? Historian Klaus Scholder explains that Germany lacked a deep democratic tradition, and would have had difficulty in forming one because German society was so thoroughly divided into opposing Protestant and Catholic blocs. This division:

> created a climate of competition, fear and prejudice between the confessions, which burdened all German domestic and foreign policies with an ideological element of incalculable weight and extent. This climate erected an almost insurmountable barrier to the formation of broad democratic center. And it favored the rise of Hitler, since ultimately both churches courted his favor—each fearing that the other would complete the Reformation or the Counter-Reformation through Hitler.[24]

Carefully plotting his strategy, Hitler purged some of the Volkish Nazi radicals most belligerent toward the traditional Christian churches. In this way he lessened the risk of ecclesiastical opposition. At the same time, he knew that the presence of both Catholics and Protestants among the Nazi leadership would ease churchmen's fears that the Party might engage in sectarianism.

Though it had many Catholic leaders (including Hitler), the Nazi Party relied heavily on Protestant support. Protestants had given the Party its principal backing during the years leading up to 1933 at a level disproportionate to their national majority.[25] Evangelical youth was especially pro-Nazi. It has been estimated that as many as 90 percent of Protestant university theologians supported the Party. Indeed, the participation of so many respected Protestants gave a early, comforting air of legitimacy to the often-thuggish Party. So did the frequent sight of *Sturmabteilung* (S.A.) units marching in uniform to church.

As German life between the wars grew more desperate, some Protestant pastors explicitly defended Nazi murders of "traitors to the Volk" from the pulpit. Antifascist Protestants found themselves marginalized. The once-unlikely topic of Volkist-Protestant compatibility became the leading theological subject of the day.[26] This is less surprising when we consider that Volkism and German Protestantism were both strongly nationalistic; Lutheranism in particular had German roots.

This mirage of harmony enticed Hitler into a naïve attempt to unite the German Protestant churches into a single Volkish body under Nazi control. Launched shortly after the Nazis came to power, this project failed immediately. The evangelical sects proved as unwilling as ever to get along with one another, though much of their clergy eventually Nazified.

CATHOLICISM AND THE NAZI TAKEOVER

Ironically—but, as we shall see, for obvious reasons—Chancellor Hitler had greater initial success reaching accommodation with Roman Catholic leaders than with the Protestants. The irony lay in the fact that the Catholic Zentrum (Center) Party had been principally responsible for denying majorities to the Nazis in early elections. Although Teutonic in outlook, German Catholics had close emotional ties to Rome. As a group they were somewhat less nationalistic than most Protestants. Catholics were correspondingly more likely than Protestants to view Hitler (incorrectly) as godless, or as a neo-heathen anti-Christian. Catholic clergy consistently denounced Nazism, though they often undercut themselves by preaching traditional anti-Semitism at the same time.

Even so, and despite Catholicism's minority status, it would be German Catholics and the Roman Catholic Church that whose actions would at last put total power within the Nazis' reach.

Though it was not without antimodernists, the Catholic Zentrum party had antagonized the Vatican during the 1920s by forming governing coalitions with the secularized, moderate Left-oriented Social Democrats. This changed in 1928, when the priest Ludwig Kaas became the first cleric to head the party. To the dismay of some Catholics, Kaas and other Catholic politicians participated both actively and passively in destroying democratic rule, and in particular the Zentrum.

The devoutly Catholic chancellor Franz von Papen, not a fascist but stoutly right-wing, engineered the key electoral victory that brought Hitler to power. Disastrously Papen dissolved the Reichstag in 1932, then formed a Zentrum-Nazi coalition in violation of all previous principles. It was Papen who in 1933 made Hitler chancellor, Papen stepping down to the vice chancellorship.

The common claim that Papen acted in the hope that the Nazis could be controlled and ultimately discredited may be true, partly true, or false; but without Papen's reckless aid, Hitler would not have become Germany's leader.

The church congratulated Hitler on his assumption of power. German bishops released a statement that wiped out past criticism of Nazism by proclaiming the new regime acceptable, then followed doctrine by ordering the laity to be loyal to this regime just as they had commanded loyalty to previous regimes. Since Catholics had been instrumental in bringing Hitler to power and served in his cabinet, the bishops had little choice but to collaborate.

German Catholics were stunned by the magnitude and suddenness of this realignment. The rigidly conformist church had flipped from ordering its flock to oppose the Nazis to commanding cooperation. A minority among German Catholics was appalled and disheartened. But most "received the statement with relief—indeed with rejoicing—because it finally also cleared the way into the Third Reich for Catholic Christians" alongside millions of Protestants, who joined in exulting that the dream of a Nazi-Catholic-Protestant nationalist alliance had been achieved.[27] The Catholic vote for the Nazis *increased* in the last multi-party elections after Hitler assumed control, doubling in some areas, inspiring a mass Catholic exodus from the Zentrum to the fascists. After the Reichstag fire, the Zentrum voted *en masse* to support the infamous Enabling Act, which would give the Hitler-Papen cabinet executive and legislative authority independent of the German Parliament. Zentrum's bloc vote cemented the two-thirds majority needed to pass the Act.

Why did the church direct its party to provide the critical swing vote? It had its agenda, as we shall see below.

DEAL MAKING WITH THE DEVIL

Even after the Enabling Act, Hitler's position remained tenuous. The Nazis needed to deepen majority popular support and cement relations with a skeptical German military. Hitler needed to ally all Aryans under the swastika while he undermined and demoralized regime opponents. What would solidify Hitler's position? A foreign policy coup: the Concordat of 1933 between Nazi Germany and the Vatican.

The national and international legitimacy Hitler would gain

through this treaty was incalculable. Failure to secure it after intense and openly promoted effort could have been a crushing humiliation. Hitler put exceptional effort into the project. He courted the Holy See, emphasizing his own Christianity, simultaneously striving to intimidate the Vatican with demonstrations of his swelling power.

Catholic apologists describe the Concordat of 1933 as a necessary move by a church desperate to protect itself against a violent regime which forced the accord upon it—passing over the contradiction at the heart of this argument. Actually, having failed in repeated attempts to negotiate the ardently desired concordat with a skeptical Weimar democracy, Kaas, Papen, the future Pius XII (who reigned 1939–1958), the sitting Pius XI, and other leading Catholics saw their chance to get what they had been seeking from an agreeable member of the church—that is, Hitler—at an historical moment when he and fascism in general were regarded as a natural ally by many Catholic leaders.[28] Negotiations were initiated by both sides, modeled on the mutually advantageous 1929 concordat between Mussolini and the Vatican.

Now Zentrum's pivotal role in assuring passage of the Enabling Act can be seen in context. It was part of the tacit Nazi-Vatican

"I may not be a light of the church, a pulpiteer, but deep down I am a pious man, and believe that whoever fights bravely in defense of the natural laws framed by God and never capitulates will never be deserted by the lawgiver, but will, in the end, receive the blessings of Providence."

—*Hitler, in a 1944 speech*

"Führer, my Führer, bequeathed to me by the Lord."

— *Prelunch invocation of German school children*

deal for a future concordat.[29] The Enabling Act vote hollowed Zentrum, leaving little more than a shell. Thus, a clergy far more interested in church power than democratic politics could take control on both sides of the negotiating table. In a flagrant conflict of interest, the devout Papen helped to represent the German state. Concordat negotiations were largely held in Rome, so that Kaas could leave his vanishing party yet more rudderless. Papen, Kaas, and the future Pius XII worked overtime to finalize a treaty that would, among other things, put an end to the Zentrum. In negotiating away the party he led, Kaas eliminated the last political entity that might have opposed the new Führer.[30] Nor did the Vatican protect Germany's Catholic party. Contrary to the contention of some, evidence indicates that the Vatican was pleased to negotiate away all traces of the Zentrum, for which it had no more use save as a bargaining chip. In this the Holy See treated Zentrum no differently than it had the Italian Catholic party, which it negotiated away in the Concordat with Mussolini.

Hitler sought to eliminate Catholic opposition in favor of obligatory loyalty to his regime. For its part, the church was obsessed with its educational privileges,[31] and especially with securing fresh sources of income. It would willingly sacrifice political power to protect them. As both sides worked in haste to produce a treaty that would normally have required years to complete, Hitler took masterful advantage of Vatican overeagerness. Filled with "certainty that Rome neither could nor would turn back, [Hitler] was now able

"The Third Reich is the first world power which not only acknowledges but also puts into practice the high principles of the papacy."

— *From Papen, who made Hitler chancellor and helped negotiate the Concordat of 1933*

> "It is to be hoped and desired that, like the Zentrum, and the Bavarian People's Party, so too the other parties which stand on Christian principles and which now also include the National Socialist Party, now the strongest party in the Reichstag, will use every means to hold off the cultural Bolshevising of Germany, which is on the march behind the Communist Party."
>
> — *Views of the future Pius XII to Cardinal Ritter after the 1932 elections*

to steer the negotiations almost as he wanted. The records prove he exploited the situation to the full."[32] Indeed, Hitler was so confident that he had the Church in his lap that he went ahead and promulgated his notorious sterilization decree *before* the Concordat's final signing. Hitler's project for involuntary sterilization of minorities and the mentally ill was a direct affront to Catholic teaching. But as Hitler surmised, not even this provocation could deflect the Holy See in its rush toward the Concordat. Because ordinary Catholics largely supported the Nazis, the party even felt free to use violence against the remaining politically active Catholics, frequently disrupting their rallies.

Signed on July 20, 1933, the Concordat was a *fait accompli*, the negotiations having been conducted largely in secret. Most German bishops gave their loyal, though impotent, approval to the pact that would strip away their power. A few bishops objected, criticizing the Nazi regime's lack of morality (but never its lack of democracy).

The Concordat was a classic political kickback scheme. The church supported the new dictatorship by endorsing the end of democracy and free speech. In addition it bound its bishops to Hitler's Reich by means of a loyalty oath. In exchange the church received enormous tax income and protection for church privileges. Religious instruction and prayer in school were reinstated.

Criticism of the church was forbidden. Of course, nothing in the Concordat protected the rights of non-Catholics.

If Catholic officials were disappointed with the Concordat's terms, they did not show it, sending messages of congratulation to the dictator. In Rome, a celebratory mass followed the treaty's signing by Papen and the future Pius XII amid great pomp and circumstance. In Germany, the church and the Berlin government held a joint service of thanksgiving that featured a mix of Catholic, Reich, and swastika banners and flags. The musical program mixed hymns with a rousing performance of the repugnant Nazi anthem "Horst Wessel"—which was set, by the way, to the traditional hymn "How Great Thou Art." All of this was projected by loudspeaker to the enthusiastic crowd outside; as most German Catholics welcomed the Concordat, the thanksgiving service drew far more than Berlin's cathedral could hold.

Scholder comments that "anyone who saw things from the Roman perspective could come to the conclusion that . . . the treaty was . . . an indescribable success for Catholicism. Even a year before, the Holy See had only been able to dream of the concessions which the concordat contained. . . . On the Catholic side the concordat was accordingly described as 'something very great,' indeed as nothing short of a 'masterpiece.'"[33] Catholic response was so exuberant that Hitler felt it necessary to defend himself to Protestant clerics and Nazi radicals who viewed this sudden amity with Rome as a betrayal.

The practical results of the collaboration were clear enough. Most Catholics "soon adjusted to the dictatorship"[34]; indeed they flocked to the Party. Post-Concordat voting patterns suggest that Catholics, on average, even outdid Protestants in supporting the regime, further undermining any efforts by the clergy to challenge Nazi policies. In any case much of the Catholic clergy was Nazifying. Even the idiosyncratic S.S. welcomed Catholics, who would ultimately compose a quarter of its membership.

The Concordat's disastrous consequences cannot be exaggerated. It bound all devout German Catholics to the state—the clergy through an oath and income, the laity through the authority of the church. If at any time the regime chose not to honor the agreement, Catholics had no open legal right to oppose it or its policies. Opponents of Nazism, Catholic and non-Catholic, were further discouraged and marginalized because the church had shown such want of moral fiber and consistency.

Apologists have insisted that the church had no choice but to accept the Concordat for the modest protections it provided. But those provisions were never needed. Major Protestant denominations suffered no more than Catholicism, though the Protestant churches lacked protective agreements and had snubbed Hitler's early attempt to unite them. Apologists make much of Vatican "resistance" to Nazism, but the net effect of Vatican policy toward Hitler was collaborative.

Indeed, the 1933 Concordat stands as one of the most unethical, corrupt, duplicitous, and dangerous agreements ever forged between two authoritarian powers. Perhaps the Catholic strategy was to outlast the Nazi's frankly popular tyranny rather than try to bring it down. But the Catholic Church made no attempt to revoke the Concordat and its loyalty clause during the Nazi regime. Indeed, the 1933 Concordat is the *only* diplomatic accord negotiated with the Nazi regime that remains in force anywhere in the world.

Germany's Protestant sects were too decentralized to be coopted by a single document. To this extent Protestants who disputed Nazi policies could be said to enjoy a more favorable position than

Catholics. But opposition was rare among Protestants too. Hitler cynically courted the major denominations even as they cynically courted him. Most smaller traditional Christian sects did little better. For example, Germany's Mormons and Seventh-Day Adventists bent over backwards to accommodate National Socialism.[35]

CHRISTIAN COMFORT WITH THE RISING REGIME

Catholics and Protestants at first embraced the new German order. Germany was regaining international prestige, the economy improving thanks to growing overseas support.[36] Industrialists like Henry Ford invested heavily in the new Reich. German Christians also looked to the Nazis for a revival of "Christian" values to help counter the rise of nontheism. Most welcomed the Nazis' elimination of chronic public strife by terrorizing, imprisoning, and killing the fast-shrinking German Left. The leftists had long been despised by traditionalists, who composed four fifths of the population. The state purged a far higher proportion of atheists than traditional Christians. In newspapers and newsreels the Nazis proudly publicized their new concentration camps. Reports sanitized the camps' true nature, but no one could mistake that they were part of a new police state—to which most German followers of Jesus raised no objection. The very high rate of "legal" executions reported in the press also met with mass indifference or positive approval.

Far from being hapless victims, the great bulk of German Christians joined, eagerly supported, collaborated with, or accommodated to a greater or lesser degree, the new tyranny.

HITLER: THE POPULAR OPPRESSOR

Apologists for Christian conduct during the Nazi era imagine that the regime suppressed dissent ruthlessly, no matter whom—or how many—it needed to slaughter to achieve its ends. Hitler's regime is portrayed as Stalinesque in its response to dissent. This simplistic view reveals a failure to understand the complicated actuality of a popular terror state. The keyword is *popular*: Hitler was Europe's most popular leader, and his goal was universal Aryan support. The Party obsessively tracked public opinion, something never seen in the USSR.[37] Before the war, foreign tourism was encouraged; Hitler knew most Germans would speak well of the Reich to visitors, in sharp contrast to the USSR, whose leaders prudently feared interaction between foreigners and a citizenry of dubious loyalty. During most of the Reich, any unprovoked attempt to liberate Germany would have met fierce majority resistance.

Though there were assassination attempts, the top Nazis had little to fear from ordinary Germans.[38] Hitler's personal security was shockingly lax; Goering regularly drove his open convertible around Berlin.

If the apologists were right, we should expect the Gestapo to have been a massive organization, relentlessly searching out and crushing widespread dissent. Analysis of surviving Gestapo records reveals that in fact it was surprisingly small.[39] Germany's Christian population being largely satisfied, there was little resistance to suppress. Most cases the Gestapo handled were initiated by ordinary citizens looking to settle petty disputes and had no ideological content.

The Führer had been successful in buying off his Aryans with false egalitarian prosperity, stolen Jewish wealth, and his refusal to put Deutschland on a full war footing until well into the war. During the early war years, civilians were under much tighter control in submarine-blockaded England than in Germany. Since nearly all Aryans were Protestant and Catholic, Hitler had to keep both sects reasonably happy, and he did. After all, the main focus of Nationalist Socialism was to make the divinely favored Aryan Volk, both Protestant and Catholic, thrive in order to transform the German population into a unified machine of domination over the lesser peoples. Contrary to Catholic apologists, the nominally Catholic Hitler had not the slightest desire to slaughter masses of the very Aryan people to whom he belonged, and whom he wanted to elevate to supreme power. Leaving aside the fact that doing so would have been ideological and racial suicide, the record makes clear that Hitler's intention was to reform and standardize Aryans' political, social, and ultimately their religious beliefs, not to purge them or to kill off groups of Aryans. Doing that would have grossly violated Nazi doctrine, undermined the myth of Aryan solidarity, grievously weakened the state, and risked religious civil war. Disloyalty of the Catholic third of the population would have been disastrous to a modest-sized nation trying to expand its resources in preparation for epic wars of conquest; it was this fact, not the Concordat, that would be the main constraint on Nazi actions. For that reason, apologist claims that thousands or millions of Catholics and Protestants would have joined the Jews had they protested Nazis policies are false. The proof is found in the historical record.

ROSENSTRASSE: THE POWER OF RESISTANCE

Far from exercising absolute power at home, Hitler often discontinued, modified, or concealed initiatives that threatened his regime's precious popular approval. Stout public objection could and repeatedly did alter Nazi behavior. Flummoxed when the Protestant churches refused to unite, Hitler deferred his grand effort to reform German Christianity to a dreamlike utopian future. Later attempts by Nazi authorities to hamper church activities were often frustrated by sizeable demonstrations.[40] When Party elements stripped Bavarian schools of their crucifixes without Hitler's approval, vigorous protests by, among others, the mothers of schoolchildren quickly brought about their replacement.[41] When Hitler denounced Protestant opposition bishops Hans Meiser and Theophil Wurm and ordered their ouster, public anger boiled over. One protest drew 7,000 demonstrators. Hitler reversed course and reinstated Meiser and Wurm with fulsome praise. Strong opposition to the mass killing of the mentally disabled *circa* 1941 drove it further underground, saving many lives, even though this program too enjoyed the Führer's approval.

This is not to say that protesters courted no danger. Opposition figures were frequently harassed, sometimes killed. But the top Nazis knew how limited their power was. When regime officials contemplated forcing the removal of Muenster's Catholic bishop, Clemens Galen, Goebbels warned that the "the population of Muenster could be regarded as lost during the war if anything were done against the bishop . . . [indeed] the whole of [the state] of Westphalia."[42] Though Galen suffered harassment, he remained

"His Holiness Pope Pius XI and the President of the German Reich, moved by a common desire to consolidate and enhance the friendly relations existing between the Holy See and the German Reich . . . have agreed to the following articles."

— *Opening of the 1933 concordat between the Holy See and Hitler's Reich*

"God gave the savior to the German people. We have faith, deep and unshakeable faith, that (Hitler) was sent by God to save Germany."

— *Goering*

active throughout the war and held his office.

In occupied countries from Norway to Italy, residents successfully opposed Nazi racial policies and saved hundreds of thousands of Jews. In Denmark, political and ecclesiastical leaders forcefully protested Nazi policies; the whole nation worked under the noses of the Gestapo to save almost all of Denmark's Jews. Neither leaders or citizens suffered severe retaliation. French bishops who opposed Nazi actions against Jews likewise survived the war.

Most extraordinary and telling is the Rosenstrasse incident.[43] Some 30,000 Jews lived openly in Germany as the spouses of Christians. Nine in ten such marriages remained intact despite ceaseless harassment. Oriented toward family values as they were, the Nazis could not decide how to handle these Jews without violating the sanctity of marriage. Early in 1943, Goebbels, then in charge of Berlin, decided it was time to cleanse the capital by rounding up these last Jews. Hitler agreed. Some 2,000 Jewish men from mixed marriages were seized and taken to a large downtown building on the Rosenstrasse, from which they would be deported to the camps.

For a week their Gentile wives stood in the winter cold, chanting "We want our husbands back!" Ordinary Germans sometimes joined them. All told, the protests involved about 6,000 people. They continued in the face of S.S. and Gestapo threats, even threats to use machine guns. They continued though British bombers pounded the city by night. But the Nazis dared not fire upon these defenseless, unorganized Aryan women. Berliners saw the protests directly. Foreign diplomats spread word of it to the world press. The British Broadcasting Company broadcast the story back into Germany.

What was the outcome of Nazi Germany's only mass demonstration to save Jews? The 2,000 Jewish husbands were released with Hitler's approval. Two dozen who had already been sent to Auschwitz were returned. Jewish-Christian couples continued to live openly and survived the war. They would comprise the great majority of German Jewish survivors.

Goebbels later commented to an associate that the regime relented "in order to eliminate the protest from the world, so that others didn't begin to do the same." Sadly, this strategy was successful: during the rest of the war, no similar action would ever be taken in defense of Jews in general.

Nor does this exhaust the catalogue of successful opposition. When Goebbels called for mass employment of housewives in war industries, also early in 1943, refusal was widespread. Again, reprisals were rare, partly because of the regime's established emphasis on traditional roles for women. On a broader scale, Germans who refused to participate in atrocities—even if they were soldiers, party members, or S.S. men—almost never suffered retaliation. This was so well known that, after the war, Nazis accused of war crimes were forbidden to claim fear of retaliation as a defense.

These incidents suggest that the Nazi regime was at root cowardly, happy to pick on the weak and disorganized but intimidated by public demonstrations. When it came to the *Volk*, Nazi leaders preferred propaganda, education, persuasion, and social pressure to terror. They knew that terror worked best when its objective was supported by many and opposed by few. Only toward the end of the war was widespread domestic terror resorted to in Germany, and it was often ineffective.

Clearly ordinary citizens *could* oppose and alter state policy, all the more so if powerful nongovernemental institutions supported them.[44] As Sarah Gordon comments, the "failure of German churches to speak out against racial persecution is a disgrace . . .

because the Nazis feared the propaganda or political power of the churches, it is almost certain that church leaders could have spoken out more vehemently against racial persecution."[45] The apologist claim that Germany's traditional Christians were impotent in the face of Nazi terror is an exaggeration on a scale that Goebbels might have appreciated. As the wives of Berlin discovered, Christians had the power to protect the lives and well-being of others and the potential to confound Hitler and his minions. Had they wished to, they need only have applied it.

Notes

1. Nazism and fascism are considered secular, atheistic, or both, in, among other sources, David Barrett, George Kurian, and Todd Johnson, eds., *World Christian Encyclopedia: A Comparative Study of Churches and Religions in the Modern World* (Oxford: Oxford University Press, 2001).

2. Seminal studies by mainstream, nonpolemical researchers include Robert Gellately, *Backing Hitler: Consent and Coercion in Nazi Germany* (Oxford: Oxford University Press, 2001); Ian Kershaw, *Hitler: 1889–1936: Hubris* (New York: W W Norton, 1998) and *Hitler: 1936–1945: Nemesis* (London: Allen Lane, 2000); Klaus Scholder, *The Churches and the Third Reich* vols. 1 and 2 (Philadelphia: Fortress Press, 1979 [English version, 1988]); Nathan Stoltzfus, *Resistance of the Heart: The Rosenstrasse Protest and Intermarriage in Nazi Germany* (New York: W.W. Norton, 1997); Beth Griech-Polelle, *Bishop von Galen: German Catholicism and National Socialism* (New Haven: Yale University Press, 2002); and Sarah Gordon, *Hitler, Germans, and the "Jewish Question"* (Princeton: Princeton University Press, 1984). Also see John Patrick Michael Murphy, "Hitler Was Not an Atheist," *Free Inquiry* 19, no. 2 (Spring 1999).

3. See James Carroll, *Constantine's Sword: The Church and the Jews* (New York: Houghton Mifflin, 2001) and David Kertzer, *The Pope Against the Jews: The Vatican's Role in the Rise of Modern Anti-Semitism* (New York: Alfred A. Knopf, 2001).

4. http://www.us-israel.org/jsource/Judaism/jewpop.html.

5. Viewed in the context of more than 1,500 years of Christian violence against Jews, the enormity of the Holocaust may as much reflect the large populations and relatively advanced technologies of the time as it does the virulence of Nazi anti-Semitism. Other Christian groups might have done the same thing earlier, had the technical means and a large enough pool of potential victims been available.

6. Nowadays Islamic anti-Semites reprint Luther's work.

7. Prior to World War I, many religious Germans viewed dying for the Fatherland as being on a par with Christian martyrdom; reluctance to die in battle was considered blasphemous.

8. After Vatican I, the Roman Catholic clergy was required to take an oath against modernity.

9. Aryan Christianity continues to exist; contemporary U.S. examples include Christian Identity, Aryan Nation, and other extremist racist sects.

10. In Aryan Christian doctrine, Christ was non-Semitic because he did not have a Jewish father. His assault on the Temple was taken as evidence of his anti-Semitism. Christianity's false association with Judaism was blamed on St. Paul.

11. Thus the extremist Christian term *mud people*. Jews' lack of a soul was held to explain their supposed lack of interest in spirituality and the afterlife and their focus on material gain.

12. For example, the Catholic Volkist Dietrich Eckart, later a friend and mentor to Hitler, wrote in 1917 that "to be an Aryan and to sense transcendence is one and the same thing," yet described Nietzsche as the "crazy despiser of our religious foundations."

13. Gregory Paul, "The Secular Revolution of the West: It's Passed America By—So Far," *Free Inquiry* 22, no. 3 (Summer 2002).

14. Ibid.

15. See Scholder vol. 1., p.12.

16. Richard Steigmann-Gall, *The Holy Reich: Nazi Conceptions of Christianity 1919–1945* (Cambridge, U.K.: Cambridge University Press, 2003) is the first attempt to detail the religious beliefs of the Nazis.

17. Christian defenders frequently cite *Table Talk*, which presents some of Hitler's most vehement anti-Christian statements. But mainstream historians find *Table Talk* unreliable. It consists of private conversations recorded in the 1940s by two secretaries, one of whom later said that "no confidence" should be placed in the final volume because the compiler—Bormann, even by Nazi standards a deceptive opportunist and much more anti-Christian than Hitler—destroyed the original transcripts. Still, even as presented in *Table Talk*, Hitler usually attacks Judeo-Christianity, not Christ. Hitler lauds Christ as a divine Aryan.

18. Timothy Ryback, "Hitler's Forgotten Library," *Atlantic Monthly* 29, no. 4 (May 2003), expresses naïve surprise at how interested Hitler was in reading about religion. Oddly, Ryback's conclusion, that Hitler saw himself as God, is contrary to the quote Ryback cites in support of his hypothesis.

19. The regime put an original edition of *On the Jews and Their Lies* on display and celebrated Luther's 450th birthday in 1933 on massive scale.

20. See Steigman-Gall.

21. Neopaganism was far more prevalent in the S.S. than in German society

as a whole; even according to Party statistics, paganism never claimed more than 5 percent of the general population.

22. See Steigman-Gall.

23. Contrary to common belief, the Nazis never operated state sex-for-procreation facilities. On the other hand, Nazi "culture" was not exceptionally prudish; home movies of the era show young women lying topless on the beach, and kitsch nudity was common in Nazi art.

24. Scholder vol. 1, p. 130.

25. See Scholder vols. 1 and 2, Kershaw pp. 488–90 and 324, and Gellately p. 14, whose *Backing Hitler* is a precedent-setting historical examination based in part on examination of surviving Gestapo records. Religion was not a primary focus of the study, but what Gellately includes on this topic is damning. See also Gordon, who gives a balanced account of church collaboration and resistance.

26. See Scholder vol. 1, pp. 37–51 and 74–87.

27. Ibid., p. 253.

28. Ronald Rychlak, "Goldhagen v. Pius XII," *First Things*, June/July 2002, pp. 37–54, offers a typically convoluted example of pro-Vatican spin when he asserts that the concordat "was a Nazi proposition. The Nazis accepted terms that the Church had previously proposed to Weimar, but which Weimar had rejected."

29. See Scholder vol. 1, p. 241.

30. Ibid., pp. 241–43.

31. A concordat already negotiated with Bavaria gave the church control of the schools.

32. Scholder vol. 1, p. 386.

33. Ibid., p. 405.

34. Gellately, p. 14.

35. See Christine Elizabeth King, *The Nazi State and the New Religions* (New York: Edwin Mellen Press, 1982).

36. Hitler and his fellow thugs had no idea how to run a modern economy. The Nazi economic "miracle" was a Potemkin-village scheme kept going, prior to the takeovers of other nations, by selling off Germany's gold reserves and taking out international loans that could never be paid back.

37. See Gellately.

38. Hitler missed by minutes being killed by a bomb a few months after invading Poland. Pope Pius XII sent the Führer his "special personal congratulations."

39. See Gellately, p. 39.

40. See Griech-Polelle, pp. 36–37.

41. Nazi politics were as peculiar as its theology. Hitler avoided committing himself on tangential issues to protect his popularity and keep his options open. This, coupled with Hitler's harsh survival-of-the-fittest view of power, fu-

eled chronic, often vicious intraparty battles that contributed to the chaos of the regime. In "working towards the Führer," party functionaries often went beyond what Hitler wanted done, at least in the short term; the Bavarian crucifix debacle is a good example of this tendency.

42. Cited in Gellately, Kershaw, p. 429, and Gordon.

43. See Stoltzfus, pp. 209–57.

44. Hitler fared little better in international affairs; even when he was master of continental Europe, his power had limits. His supposed ally Franco politely told the vexed Führer to take a hike when he pressed for Spain to enter the war against the allies. Hitler found himself forced to negotiate with the Vichy French government he had helped to install over the same matter, and it too refused to budge.

45. Gordon, p. 261.

The complete compilation of excerpts from material linking Christianity and Nazism (featured in boxed quotations here) is available on the Web at www.secularhumanism.org/index.php/ articles/3020. Tim Binga, director of the Center for Inquiry Libraries, contributed additional research in the preparation of this article.

Gregory S. Paul is an independent evolutionary scientist and paleontologist with interests in the relationship between science and religion. His books include Dinosaurs of the Air *(Johns Hopkins University Press) and* Beyond Humanity *(coauthor Earl Cox, Charles River Media, 1996).*

THE GREAT SCANDAL
PART 2
CHRISTIANITY'S ROLE IN THE RISE OF THE NAZIS
Gregory S. Paul

In the first part of this article, Gregory S. Paul probed the foundations of Christian anti-Semitism from the early church through Martin Luther into the twentieth century. By the 1920s, several distinct religious strands allied and battled with one another in Germany. Protestantism and Catholicism (collectively, "traditional Christianity") remained strongly antimodern and anti-Semitic. Aryan Christians were fierce racial anti-Semites who denied that Christ was a Jew. Aryan neopaganism blended Germanic bombast with Norse myth and rejected Christianity because Christ was Jewish. Collectively Aryan Christianity and paganism comprised Volkism, fount of Nazi myth and doctrine. Still, neopagan influence was modest compared to Christianity's. Contrary to some Christian apologists, atheism played no role in the rise of the Nazis.

All principal Nazi leaders were Protestant or Catholic by birth. Hitler's religious views were complex. A nominal Catholic who neither disavowed his faith nor was excommunicated, his mature beliefs included Christ as his Savior, alongside a conviction that annihilating the racial enemies of the Volk was God's work. Hitler publicly and privately condemned atheism and boasted of stamping it out. He hoped to subsume existing Protestantism and

Catholicism into a reformed church free of Jewish and Roman influence. Occult and neopagan influences on Hitler were minimal. Instead he saw himself not as Christianity's enemy but its ultimate reformer.

The Nazi takeover required Christian collaboration. It was welcomed by a German majority who disdained the Weimar Republic. Germany's Catholics would give the Nazis ultimate power. Devout Catholic chancellor Franz von Papen engineered Hitler's electoral victory and brokered a coalition between the Nazi Party and the formerly anti-Nazi Catholic party, the Zentrum. Zentrum was ultimately destroyed by its head, Ludwig Kaas, a priest who drafted the infamous 1933 Concordat between Hitler and the Vatican (alongside Papen and the future Pope Pius XII). The Concordat subjected German Catholics to Nazi authority in return for various benefits, including extravagant financial transfers to the Roman Church.

Hitler was very popular; few religious leaders resisted Nazi initiatives. Contrary to claims that Hitler relied primarily on terror to cow domestic opposition, he curried public opinion, repeatedly backpedaled in the face of popular outrage, and eschewed using mass force against his volk. *When Nazi zealots stripped crucifixes from Bavarian schools, widespread protest persuaded Hitler to order them replaced. Numerous German housewives defied a 1943 campaign to employ them in war industries, without reprisals. The same year Goebbels detained some two thousand Jewish Berlin men married to Christian women. For a week the Gentile wives stood before the holding center on the Rosenstrasse chanting, "We want our husbands back!" Fearing public embarrassment, Goebbels and Hitler avoided crushing the protesters as the Jews were released. Meanwhile, despite being Hitler's small dependent ally, the democratic Finnish government firmly refused to cooper-*

*ate with Nazi wishes to deport the nation's Jews, and none were
harmed.*

*Defenders of Christian behavior under the Nazis face a di-
lemma: If Berlin housewives could openly oppose the Führer's
racial policies—if willful Scandinavians could defy the greatest
military empire—how much further horror might have been averted
had millions of Catholics and Protestants consistently opposed the
Nazis?—*EDS.

THE GYRE OF CONFUSION

The relationship between Nazis and the churches was schizo-
phrenic at best. Hitler dutifully paid the religious taxes he had in-
stituted while he disparaged and schemed against the clergy those
taxes supported. The party that once plucked crosses from schools
it had encouraged to teach religion also held rallies in Christian
venues blazoned with crosses. Nazi literature frequently set cross
and swastika side by side. Then again, Hermann Goering declared
that the Nazi stiff-arm should be considered "the only salute to
Christ." Some religious schools and monasteries were harassed,
even closed, and church property confiscated; others were protected by the regime. The newly crowned Pope Pius XII protested
one such round of closings and dabbled in a plot against Hitler's
rule. Yet he sent the Führer fawning greetings, and cheerful birthday messages yearly.[1]

Other figures in our narrative exemplify this same confusion.
Among the politicians, consider Franz von Papen. A year after
helping Hitler to power, he criticized the party and barely escaped
with his life. Yet he went on to give the Nazis good service as special minister to Austria, and later as ambassador to strategic Turkey
(1939–44). After the war Papen was acquitted at Nuremberg, but

convicted by a denazification court—the sentence was overturned under pressure from Papen's church.

Among the clergy, consider Bishop Clemens Galen. Often touted as a Hitler opponent, the "Lion of Muenster" was an ardent nationalist who detested democracy and allowed uniformed *Schutzstaffel* (S.S.) and *Sturmabteilung* (S.A.) members into his consecration procession. Although he sometimes criticized Aryan racism, Galen offered no response to Kristallnacht, and often removed references to Jews when quoting from the Bible. In July and August 1941, he preached three famous sermons against Nazi power, but they focused almost entirely on Gestapo attacks against the church. In one sermon Galen denounced Hitler's euthanasia project, but he never decried the plight of minorities or urged Catholics to aid them. Quite the contrary, he described the Jewish people as "the only one that rejected God's truth, that threw off God's law and so condemned itself to ruin" (a passage Catholic defenders rarely republish) and exhorted Catholics to "fight and die for Germany." Galen never discussed the Holocaust nor objected to Jews being deported from his diocese. In 1943 he gave a pro-war sermon later used by the Nazis to recruit for the S.S. After the war he called the Nuremberg proceedings "show trials."

One feels sympathy for those Germans who questioned the decency of the Nazi regime, as their men of God led them in confusing circles of moral relativity and ethical depravity.

THE MARCH OF ANTI-SEMITISM

Though Jews had won substantial acceptance in Germany prior to 1933, the Nazis had little difficulty fanning anti-Semitism to pogrom heat. This was possible only because traditional Christianity furnished the foundation Nazi ideologues could build on.[2]

"Christianity in Germany bears a greater responsibility before God than
the National Socialists, the SS, and the Gestapo."
— *Observation by Martin Niemöller*
(in Hitler's Willing Executioners, *Daniel Goldhagen, p. 114)*

If anything, records show, anti-Semitism tended to be higher
among more religious Germans.[3] Many Protestant bishops openly
supported fascist racial policies, leading to a notorious group proc-
lamation to that effect in 1941. Across Germany, lay Protestants
were anti-Semitic in varying degrees: moderates favored voluntary
conversion to solve the "Jewish problem," while Volkish hardlin-
ers thought elimination the only way to deal with the Semites.

As for Catholics, the fact that a small minority occasionally
rescued Jews no more proves their lack of bigotry than would the
sight of Southern segregationists rescuing Blacks from a flood.[4]
More telling, as the Holocaust loomed and later raged, Pius XII and
the church he ruled went on promulgating the view that Judaism
was defective. In the same vein, when Archbishop Bertram voiced
opposition to the proposed forced divorce of Catholics and Jews in
1942, he hastened to caution that he was not minimizing the "harm-
ful Jewish influences upon German cultural and national interests."

Apologists point to the hundreds of thousands of Jews saved
by valiant Protestant and Catholic clergy throughout occupied
Europe—among them the future Pope John XXIII, a true friend to
the Jews. Although laudable, the hard truth is that by 1945 80 percent of Europe's Jews were dead, their community all but cleansed
at the hands of people of Christian faith or heritage.

Though ordinary Germans varied in the depth of their racism,
most understood that their country had become inconceivably
brutal. Much as Americans once mailed postcards of lynchings,[5]

Germans hoarded still photos and motion pictures of atrocities in private and official troves. Drawing on this material, Gellately recounts the massive use of slave labor in German war industries. In many locales, sick and deliberately ill-fed slaves were marched to and from work in open view of citizens, who could scarcely avoid seeing the slaves' wretched condition. Survivors recount occasional sympathy and assistance, but the usual reaction of ordinary Germans was indifference, disgust, or hostility.

The Holocaust could not have happened without Hitler. But it also could not have happened without traditional Christianity. Hitler was no Buddhist, nor a secular humanist.

WERE TRADITIONAL CHRISTIANS MASS-MURDERED?

Christian defenders assert that believers also faced Nazi persecution for their beliefs. However, the numbers were modest: Thomsett estimates that, over twelve years, about six thousand German clergy were sent to camps, of whom two thousand died.[6] And most or all were targeted for anti-Nazi activities. The scale of this horror pales compared to the ten thousand leftists arrested in Bavaria during just two *months* in 1933, or the hundreds of thousands killed throughout the Nazi period. As detailed in Part 1 of this article, Hitler valued domestic public opinion and had no wish to exterminate the people from whom he hoped to fashion a purified and reformed Aryan Christian body, free from the influence of Rome or the synagogue.

Nontraditional Christian groups could face greater peril. Germany's Jehovah's Witnesses were pacifist, pro-Zionist, small enough to be vulnerable—and harshly dealt with. When the qua-

"The Lord is a man of war." — *Exodus 15:3*

si-religious White Rose movement blossomed among students in wartime Munich, its leaders were beheaded. (As previously noted, German Mormons and Seventh-day Adventists accommodated the Nazis and were spared.[7])

On the other hand, traditional Christians of non-Aryan heritage were naked before Nazi brutality. After invading Poland, Hitler ordered most Polish priests liquidated because these Slavic members of the ruling class could help organize resistance. The pope who had negotiated the Concordat was horrified, but his birthday greetings to Hitler continued.

In truth, few observant traditional Christians went to the camps because few offered serious resistance to the regime. Jews are outraged by attempts to memorialize individual Christians lost in the horrific system, since most Catholics and Protestants in the camps were the loathsome administrators and guards. Instead of accusing the Nazis of massacring traditional Christians, they should be charged for their crimes against atheists and freethinkers, who *were* explicit targets of Nazi oppression and died in the camps in substantial numbers.

FOLLOW THE MONEY

Even more than their racist and anti-enlightened attitudes, Christian authorities had the basest of reasons to cooperate with fascists—money. Stripped of her last papal states in 1925, the Mother Church lay bankrupt until Benito Mussolini came to the rescue. In exchange for the pope's support, Il Duce made an up-front payment equivalent to about $100 million and instituted state salaries for the Italian clergy. Best of all, Mussolini restored Vatican City's nationhood. Today's Vatican has its roots in fascist largesse.[8]

But the pope coveted richer booty. How might he tap the far

grander wealth of Germany? No German Protestant dictator or Protestant-dominated democracy would pay tribute to Rome; no out-and-out papist could rule Deutschland. Then came the miracle: Hitler, the nonpapist Catholic who inexplicably rose from obscurity to the brink of power and—eyeing the fascist-Catholic concordat in Italy—eagerly sought similar ties with the church. Surely this was God's amazing work.

The result was one of history's richest kickback schemes. The pope gave Hitler legitimacy, his office, and the enforced loyalty of German prelates. In return, one-tenth of the income tax paid by German Catholics would flow from Hitler's treasury to the church accounts.[9] This averaged the equivalent of $100 million per year, approximately $1 billion over the life of the Third Reich—many times that in today's dollars.[10] Because the grateful pontiffs held the same absolute control over the church's funds that the Führer exercised over the German treasury, it can be fairly said that Pius XI (reigned 1922–1939) and Pius XII (reigned 1939–1958) were on Hitler's payroll.

Nor did Hitler forget his evangelical friends. Ten percent of Protestants' tax payments was diverted to *their* churches too. Hitler needed no loyalty oaths from Germany's ministers, who realized the equivalent of about $2 billion over the life of the Reich.

Flush with wealth, the churches invested heavily in fascist enterprises, many of which would manufacture weapons, employ slave labor, or both.[11] Ironically, as church leaders began to act as financiers and brokers, their prejudice against usury, ancient keystone of anti-Semitism, melted away.

It cannot be said too bluntly: a principal reason that traditional Christian clergymen, from the humblest country parson to the popes, so often cooperated with Hitler was that they were being bribed.

THE PRICE

Christendom paid for its avarice. Some 2.5 million European Protestant soldiers and civilians died; the Catholic toll, which included people from other countries where Catholics were not in the minority as they were in Germany, was broadly similar. Perhaps half of all Soviets were Orthodox, and so their Christian dead amounted to fifteen million or more. All told, more than twenty million Christians died. That probably exceeds the toll of nontheists. It far exceeds the Holocaust toll of six million Jews.

And it all could have been prevented had Europe's Christians resolved to put a stop to it.

PIUS XII AND THE HOLOCAUST

How might a meaningful Christian resistance to fascism have come about? It would never arise spontaneously; anti-democratic and anti-Semitic attitudes were too widespread. A united front against fascism would have demanded strong leadership from someone who could make clear in forthright terms what was right and what had to be done—someone who could set an inspiring ethical example and back it with moral power. With nearly half a billion adherents worldwide and a third of Germany's population, the Roman Catholic Church had the potential for enormous influence. Daring action by Pius XI, Pius XII, and other Catholic leaders could have

"In the name of the Most Holy Trinity. Whereas the Holy See and Italy have recognized the desirability of eliminating every reason for dissension existing between them . . . his Holiness the Supreme Pontiff Pius XI and . . . his Excellency the Cav. Benito Mussolini . . . have hereby agreed to the following articles."

— *Opening of the Lateran Treaty of 1929*

changed history, preserved democracy, and saved millions of lives, furnishing a shining example of Christian morality in action. But that would have meant turning off the fascist money taps.

Apologists make much of Pius XI's 1937 encyclical to German Catholics, which attacked Nazi racism. Yet it never mentioned the Jews. In 1939, Pius said Jews had access to God's grace like all others (a point he would repeat in 1943). But he undermined himself, using the same encyclical to reprise the charge that Jews bore guilt for Christ's death. "Blinded by their dream of worldly gain and material success," he proclaimed, Jews deserved "worldly and spiritual ruin."

Catholics obsess over how in one 1942 speech Pius XII included a few sentences condemning the suffering of unnamed innocents. Yet he never identified perpetrators or victims, masking his most public indictment of history's greatest slaughter as a bland statement of general principles. Viewed critically, Pius XII's 1942 Christmas statement was a minimal, ineffectual effort of the kind often made by a conflicted collaborator, who, under intense pressure from the Allies, had to put some statement on the record. Nor did he revisit the Holocaust, however obliquely, in his Christmas messages of 1943 or 1944, when the killing was at its height. Nor did he instruct the clergy or those who prepared church publications to discontinue traditional attacks on Jews as "Christ-killers." Nor did he take public action to prevent the mass transport to Auschwitz of those Italian Jews not hidden by Catholics.

The Catholic Church controlled the largest, most experienced propaganda machine in the world. Every pope understood the importance of ceaseless, drumbeat promulgation of an idea in effective campaigns. Yet so few and so feeble were Vatican thrusts against the Holocaust that apologists must scour the records to glean unconvincing scraps of evidence for Pius XII's good intentions. Given the extent of Rome's international intelligence apparatus, Pius XII must have known at least in outline what was taking place in the camps. Because of the international breadth of his organization, his neutrality, and his potential as a moral leader, he was best positioned to reveal, condemn, and act against the Holocaust. Even if he did everything his defenders contend he did to save hundreds of thousands, the fact remains that the man who considered himself the supreme arbiter of moral values on Earth proved unable to save millions more when he alone had the potential tools to get the job done. But he could not, and did not. Why?

Pius XII failed in part because he feared too much for his flock and its victims, fearing a backlash as he underestimated the church's power to bend Nazi behavior. He failed in part because, a seasoned diplomat, he held egotistic dreams of negotiating an end to the war himself. But he also failed because of Catholic doctrine, because he hated democracy as well as Bolshevism, and because he cared too little about Jews and atheists. Most of all, Pius XII failed because his church enjoyed the fascist revenue stream.

WHAT IF . . .?

Imagine not just one Rosenstrasse demonstration, but thousands. Imagine if Germany's Lutheran ministers and Catholic priests had ceaselessly preached *anti*–anti-Semitism from the pulpits. Imagine if its churches had showed the same resolve as occupied Denmark and Finland.

"I am convinced that I am acting as an agent of our Almighty creator. By warding off the Jews I am fighting for the Lord's work."

— *Hitler, in* Mein Kampf *and a 1936 speech*

If Pius XII had worn the Star of David in sympathy with the Jews, the worldwide effect would have been electric. Imagine if Pius XII had called explicitly, incessantly, for equal treatment of Jews and open international inspection of the camps. Imagine if he had consistently demanded the privilege of conducting his own personal inspection of any camp on two days' notice, with the right to interview inmates without interference. Imagine if he had called Jews and atheists his brothers and sisters, and released an encyclical commanding Catholics to do all they could to aid them.[12] Imagine if he had consistently denounced authoritarianism and aggression, perhaps undertaking a pilgrimage to Berlin to discuss the errant ways of his nominal theological subject, Adolf Hitler. The Nazis would have been tied in knots.

A regime that could not figure out how to handle obstructionist Scandinavians or outraged housewives would have had either to accommodate the pope's demands, or persuade the Italian fascists to put an end to them. The latter course would not only have destroyed Italian fascism's critical relations with the papacy, but outraged the world. Forthright papal defiance would have carried risks, but it could have disabled the Nazi extermination campaign.

Apologists try to deflect such criticisms by arguing that Pius XII was wiser to conduct secretive rescue operations rather than "endangering others with grand public gestures."[13] But great horrors require bolder action to stop them. There was no quiet way to rescue millions being destroyed by a vast machine that could only operate in secrecy; safety for protesters lay precisely in great numbers. The way to minimize both risks and losses was by just the outspoken public actions that Catholic defender Ronald Rychlak disparaged as "foolish."[14]

DON'T BLAME ATHEISM

There is blame to spare for the calamity of World War II. Some atheists supported leftist dictatorships; some scientists advocated racial eugenics and otherwise facilitated tyranny. But in no way was Nazism the invention of Europe's atheists. Their influence was severely limited and at most indirect. (To the degree that European atheists tended to support communism, they *opposed* fascism.) Nazi ideology grew and thrived in a land dominated by Christianity.

Because Nazism has left so horrific a stain on history, Christian apologists struggle to lay its causes in the lap of atheism. This is historical spin of the highest order. *Mein Kampf* never mentions evolution, Darwin, or Nietzsche. "Science" justified Nazi racism the same way pseudoscience "backs" creationism. Far from atheism spawning a Nazi machine that proceeded to assault Christianity, atheists and their organizations were targeted and destroyed while German churches not only survived, but thrived on Nazi graft. That atheists are not regularly listed with Jews, Roma, homosexuals, and other principal targets of the Holocaust betokens an ongoing injustice.

BLAME THEISM

The tragic truth is that top-ranking Nazis, as well as the German multitudes who initially supported them, were products of a traditional Christian culture that had eagerly rejected the brief Weimar experiment. It is especially meaningful that the Nazis most responsible for the Holocaust—Hitler, Himmler, Heydrich, and Hoess— all came from conservative Catholic households, steeped in obedience to clerical authority and reflexive anti-Semitism. *All* of the Nazi leaders were theists, whether Catholic, Protestant, or Aryan. Hitler's grandiose schemes flowed from a fanatical religious worldview. *Mein Kampf* is a creationist tract that repeatedly cites providence, the eternal creator, almighty lord, God, and Christ as the divine power that made most non-Aryans soulless subhumans suitable only for slavery, or worse.[15] It cannot be overemphasized that to believe that Jews were subhuman, yet ingenious enough to take over the world, was conceivable only if one regarded them as the product of diabolical supernatural forces, a concept beyond the reach of "scientific" anti-Semitism. The Holocaust was as much an act of faith as the attacks of 9/11.

A movement is best judged not by its doctrines or the goodness of its minority, but by the actions of its majority. Apologists contend that Christians failed to oppose fascism because they did not understand its true intentions or feared liquidation if they spoke out. Although sometimes true, most Continental Christians accepted, even favored, fascism because they approved of right-wing authoritarianism, approved of Nazi racial policies as they understood them, or felt that fascism's benefits outweighed the sufferings of Jews and other social outcasts. So extensive was Christian collaboration that efforts to oppose Nazism by atheists and other minorities were crushed.

We should not be surprised that a strongly Protestant and Catholic culture could so readily accommodate profound evil. Christian morality springs from the Bible, a collection of texts written by tribal peoples with primitive moral codes. From it we receive the doctrines that there is only one truth, that dissent is heresy, that slavery is acceptable. Democracy is foreign to any biblical tradition, while Scripture abounds with "final solutions" in which God brutally slaughters whole populations. Moses and Joshua are explicitly portrayed as committing genocide at God's behest.[16] Nazi propagandists could hardly cite Jewish scripture to justify their actions, but Old Testament tales of conquest influenced

Hitler, who privately cited them as a guide to his own methods. By comparison with the Old Testament, the New calls for brotherhood—but only in a doctrinal context that segregates human souls into categories of "us" and "them," the former destined for a loving but tyrannical utopia, the latter for eternal torment.

Beyond the Bible, traditional and Aryan Christians could draw on long-standing Germanic-Christian traditions of aggression, authoritarianism, and anti-Semitism. Who could oppose Jew-hating if the greatest Christian reformer (Luther) promoted it and the greatest Christian church practiced it?

Tribal and tyrannical, Nazism could thrive in a Christian culture whose obsolete doctrines provided a subtle but pervasive socio-moral tradition of mass violence and theft as a way to deal with opponents of the one true utopia. Hitler stands as the ultimate example of the dangers of education in the Bible and Christian history.

CONSEQUENCES

The world wars and the Holocaust gave Europe a spiritual shock that drove the continent to break with faith at last. Only about a quarter of today's Europeans remain devoutly Christian; a like number doubt the existence of any higher power. Demographic indicators favor continued secularization.[17] Secular forces, not the churches, are associated with resistance to fascism and anti-Semitism in the European mind. It is therefore not surprising that across today's remarkably de-Christianized, modernistic, democratic, tolerant, and hedonistic Europe, biblical-scale atrocities are limited to those enclaves where religion remains strong.[18] Less affected by the darker side of Christian doctrine and history—and hence less cognizant of them—the United States remains the only first-world nation to retain a level of religious belief seen otherwise only in the third world.[19]

After decades of refusal, the Vatican is claiming that it will release more of its Nazi-era records. This begs the question why an organization claiming nothing to hide and much to be proud of has not always followed a fully open-door policy for historical records and current accounts. Protestant involvement in fascism also demands further historical inquiry. Across the board, there is a critical need for objective, nonpolemical research into a subject that has too long been "off limits": the role of European religion in facilitating the rise of the Nazis.

If, as some apologists still claim, German Christians did the best they could, they were remarkably impotent and corruptible, the more so since courageous exposure of and opposition to Nazi atrocities could likely have ended them. The great scandal overturns Christian tales of heroic resistance to fascism and their claims to large-scale victimhood. The claim that their faith is the best and only path toward a just society is forever refuted.

Notes

1. See Ian Kershaw, *Hitler: 1889–1936: Hubris* (New York: W W Norton, 1998); Kershaw, *Hitler: 1936–1945: Nemesis* (London: Allen Lane, 2000), and Robert Gellately, *Backing Hitler: Consent and Coercion in Nazi Germany* (Oxford: Oxford University Press, 2001).

2. See James Carroll, *Constantine's Sword: The Church and the Jews* (New York: Houghton Mifflin, 2001).

3. See Gellately; also Sarah Gordon, *Hitler, Germans and the "Jewish Question"* (Princeton: Princeton University Press, 1984), p.260.

4. One priest who rescued Jews told them he disliked them but that rescuing them was "the Christian thing" to do. Marthe Cohn, *Behind Enemy Lines* (New York: Harmony, 2002).

5. Philip Dray, *At the Hands of Persons Unknown: The Lynching of Black America* (New York: Random House, 2002).

6. See Michael Thomsett, *The German Opposition to Hitler* (Jefferson: McFarland & Co, 1997), p.67.

7. See Christine Elizabeth King, *The Nazi State and the New Religions* (New York: Edwin Mellen Press, 1982), pp. 89–119.

8. See Paul Williams, *The Vatican Exposed: Money, Murder and the Mafia* (Amherst, N.Y.: Prometheus Books, 2003), pp.15–32.

9. This religious tax continues to be collected and distributed to this day (about $8 billion yearly to all sects) though increasing numbers of Germans opt out by stating no denomination.

10. Williams, op. cit.

11. Williams, op. cit.

12. In her *Bishop von Galen: German Catholicism and National Socialism* (New Haven: Yale University Press, 2002), Beth Griech-Polelle wonders whether Pius XII feared that his followers were too anti-Semitic to obey orders to help Jews. Whether or not the Catholic laity would have risen to the occasion will never be known, since their leader declined to risk the experiment.

13. Ronald Rychlak, "Goldhagen v. Pius XII," *First Things*, June/July 2002, pp. 37–54. Many less polemical researchers, such as Gordon, have also mistakenly assumed that mass protests would have been ruthlessly suppressed.

14. Ibid.

15. *Mein Kampf* was a blunt handbook for party members, not a carefully targeted recruiting tract. Some abbreviated translations expunge most of Hitler's religious comments.

16. God ordered the Israelites to exterminate the Canaanites utterly. Extensive tracts detail subsequent ethnic cleansing, annihilating millions of "man and woman, infant and suckling." These mythical accounts probably helped inspire Hitler's extermination of leftists, intellectuals, and Jews during Operation Barbarossa.

17. Gregory S. Paul, "The Secular Revolution of the West: It's Passed America By—So Far," *Free Inquiry* 22, no. 3 (Summer 2002).

18. Though secularism seems effective in suppressing atrocities, Christianity often remains helpless to prevent them. Catholic and Protestant churches proved ineffectual in Northern Ireland and the Balkans; Rwanda is the most Christian African nation with over 80 percent believers, the majority Catholic, who widely participated in the atrocities of 1996 during which clergy were either complicit or ineffectual. In particular, the pope could have flown to the scene and ordered his flock to cease participating in the killing, but chose not to do so.

19. Paul, op. cit.

The complete compilation of excerpts from material linking Christianity and Nazism (featured in sidebars here) is available on the Web at www.secularhumanism.org/index.php/articles/3020. Tim Binga, director of the Center for Inquiry Libraries, contributed additional research in the preparation of this article.

THE HARM THAT RELIGION DOES: A CASE STUDY

Peter Singer

Ever since August 2001, when President Bush announced his shaky compromise policy on federal funding for research on stem cells, American scientists have been charging that the policy severely impedes progress in this promising new area. Bush's policy allowed federal funding only for research using stem cell lines that were in existence on the date of his speech. Thus, he maintained, such funding would not encourage anyone to destroy human embryos to obtain stem cells, because if they did so, the newly created stem cell lines could not be developed or studied with federal funding.

On August 9, 2001, Bush claimed that "more than sixty genetically diverse stem cell lines already exist." Finding these stem cell lines proved difficult, however, and many of them turned out not to be suitable for research. In September 2002, Dr. Curt Civin, a stem cell researcher at Johns Hopkins University, told a congressional committee that "embryonic stem cell research is crawling like a caterpillar" and that stem cells were available "only to those persistent and patient enough to jump through a series of hoops and endure lengthy waits."[1] Subsequent reports put the number of stem cell lines that satisfied federal guidelines for funding and were useful for research at eleven. Senator Arlen

Specter, a Republican from Pennsylvania, asked President Bush to "expand" his earlier decision and make more cell lines eligible for research with federal funding. The president did not respond to this request.[2]

Last February, as if to confirm what critics had been saying, South Korean scientists revealed that they had made embryonic human clones from adult women. One of these cloned embryos had developed long enough to permit stem cells to be extracted. The technique would, in principle, make possible the development of individual stem cell lines, taken from those who are ill and would benefit from the stem cells. There would then be no problem of rejection, for the stem cells used in treating the illness would be a perfect genetic match with the cells of the person in need of the treatment. Such research could not be done with federal funding in the United States.

There are good grounds for being cautious about producing new human beings by cloning. Even if we disregard the often hysterical fears of armies of identical clones, at least in our present state of knowledge, there is too great a risk of the cloned human having serious abnormalities. But the Korean scientists were not interested in producing a human child. Their interest was only in developing the early embryo to the blastocyst stage, the point at which stem cells could be obtained. At that stage, the embryo does not have any of its subsequent anatomical features, like a backbone, limbs, or a head. It is not recognizably human or even mammalian and, lacking even the most vestigial brain or nervous system, could not possibly be a conscious being.

Nevertheless, the announcement by the South Korean scientists led to the usual chorus of denunciation from conservative religious leaders. "You can't kill human life in the hopes of finding medicines to save other lives," said Monsignor Elio Sgrecia, vice president of the Vatican's Pontifical Academy for Life and a papal advisor on matters of bioethics. Then he added: "That would be a repeat of what the Nazis did in the concentration camps."[3]

(A note in passing. When People for the Ethical Treatment of Animals [PETA] drew some parallels between the Nazi Holocaust and the mass slaughter of animals, many Jewish organizations protested, even though PETA's comparison quoted the noted Jewish writer, Isaac Bashevis Singer, making the same point. Yet Monsignor Sgrecia's much more explicit equation of the Holocaust with the destruction of very early embryos, basically groups of cells incapable of feeling anything at all, appears to have drawn no protests. One can only wonder why not.)

It is not, of course, the fact that another nation is leading the United States in research on stem cells that matters. Science is not the Olympics, and getting worried about national rankings in scientific research is absurd. What does matter is that, without U.S. funding for stem cell research, the global effort in this area moves forward more slowly, because one leading player is absent.

We need to remember how important this area of research is. A fact sheet issued by the White House—yes, President Bush's White House—has stated that: "Many scientists believe that embryonic stem cell research may eventually lead to therapies that could be used to treat diseases that afflict approximately 128 million Americans." The fact sheet goes on to mention possible treatments for Parkinson's disease, diabetes, and heart attacks, as well as advances in basic biology and testing the safety and efficacy of new medicines.[4] In other words, the stakes are huge.

No observer of American politics can doubt that, if it were not for religious opposition to the destruction of these early embryos, federal funding would be available for research in this area. If anyone ever tries to tell you that, for all its quirks and irrationality, religion is harmless or even beneficial for society, remember those 128 million Americans—and hundreds of millions more citizens of other nations—who might be helped by research that is being restricted by religious beliefs. Meanwhile, just be glad that Christians in South Korea do not have the political clout that they have in America.

Notes

1. Sheryl Stolberg, "Stem Cell Research Is Slowed by Restrictions, Scientists Say," *New York Times*, September 26, 2002.

2. Nicholas Wade, "Specter Asks Bush to Permit More Embryonic Stem Cell Lines," *New York Times*, April 23, 2003.

3. Reuters, as reported on CNN International, February 13, 2004, http://edition.cnn.com/2004/WORLD/europe/02/13/vatican.clones.reut/.

4. White House, "Fact Sheet: Embryonic Stem Cell Research," August 9, 2001, http://www.whitehouse.gov/news/releases/2001/08/20010809-1.html.

Peter Singer is the Ira W. DeCamp Professor of Bioethics at Princeton University. His new book is The President of Good and Evil: The Ethics of George W. Bush *(Dutton, 2004).*

SHOULD WE RESPECT RELIGION?

Barbara Smoker

On May 25, 2006, I took part in the Oxford University Union Debate, opposing the motion that "Free speech should be moderated by respect for religion." The chief speaker on my side was Flemming Rose, the Danish editor who published the controversial Muhammad cartoons. As there is a seven-figure bounty on his head, the security arrangements for the debate were heavy. Everyone was searched on the way in. In the days when, as president of the National Secular Society, I frequently took part in university debates (mainly during the 1970s through the 1990s). I was almost invariably on the losing side when it came to the vote, but this time we won by a good margin—129–59.

If the word *religion* in the motion were replaced by any other abstract noun, we would have won by 188 to nil. Suppose the word was *science*. The motion would then have read "Free speech should be moderated by respect for science"; and no reasonable person would vote for that—least of all a genuine scientist. So why is religion given its uniquely privileged status? After thousands of years, it is the norm—so no one ever thinks it needs justifying.

As I pointed out in the debate, the precept to respect religion is similar to the Mosaic commandment, "Honor thy Father and thy Mother." But suppose your father and mother happened to be murderers? They wouldn't deserve your respect, and most religions don't either.

Should we, then, respect religious faith? Certainly not. But should we respect religious people? Yes—as long as they are not antisocial and do not aim to impose their religious views on others.

However, even if we respect them as good-living people, we cannot respect their beliefs. Faith, which means firm belief in the absence of evidence, betrays human intelligence, undermines science-based knowledge, and compromises ordinary morality. If there were objective evidence for its doctrines, it would no longer be faith; it would be knowledge.

We have to excuse the medieval skeptics who pretended to respect Christianity rather than risk being burned at the stake, and likewise the apostate Muslims of today who pay lip-service to Islam in those Islamic countries where apostasy is still a capital offense; but we who live in a comparatively liberal society have no such excuse. In fact, it is all the more incumbent upon us to give our support to victims of religious oppression everywhere by coming out of the respectful closet and speaking our minds. Freedom of speech is more important than respect.

Skepticism is of paramount importance, because it is the gateway to knowledge; but unless the skeptical ideas are freely argued over, they cannot be assessed, nor can the ensuing knowledge spread through society.

There can be no real freedom of religion without freedom *from* religion, which is part of the whole concept of free speech. As J.S. Mill wrote, no idea can be justified unless it is open to opposition—which means free speech and free expression. And free speech must include the right to laugh at absurd ideas. Indeed, ridicule—including satirical cartoons—has always been an important element of the free exchange of ideas on everything, not least religion. Without that free exchange, there can be no advance in knowledge and no social progress. Totalitarian extremists, of whatever religion or sect, invariably put faith first and freedom nowhere. Censorship, including insidious self-censorship, is then the order of the day, followed closely by violence. In a society where religious orthodoxy rules, there is no freedom of religion.

Incidentally, the violence provoked by the Danish cartoons was deliberately stirred up by Islamic extremists publishing exaggerated versions of them in Muslim countries, up to four months after the originals were published.

I have discussed this with several moderate Muslims, and while they roundly condemned the violent reprisals, they generally added, "But people ought not to insult religion." Why *not*? No one would denounce the ridiculing of *political* views, which are open to free debate. In fact, *true* respect for religion would allow it to be opened up in the same way, relying on the truth emerging. But at present it is shielded from honest scrutiny. This suggests that the faithful realize it could not stand up to it.

We are told by politicians and mealy-mouthed functionaries that it is politically incorrect to call the perpetrators of the July 7, 2005, bombings in London Muslim terrorists—but, of course, everyone knows they *were* Muslims, of the most zealous kind. Their belief in a blissful afterlife for martyrs is another aspect of the problem, and, since this afterlife belief is unshakable, what we need perhaps is a revered ayatollah to proclaim, with Qur'anic support, that suicide bombers will actually go to hell (or, at least, that paradise has run out of virgins).

Though we must take care to avoid a native backlash against

the mostly peaceable British Muslim community, succeeding governments have carried the exoneration of Muslim villains too far in the past. For instance, as long ago as 1989, when imams were offering bribes on BBC television for the murder of Salman Rushdie, they were never charged with incitement to murder.

The July 7 suicide bombers were British-born Muslim youths, three of whom—all found dead—were quickly identified. At least one of them used to attend the Finsbury Park Mosque, where Abu Hamza was knowingly allowed, for eight years, to preach violent hatred and incite young men to murder, before the Crown Prosecution Service started criminal proceedings against him in 2004—and only then because the United States was demanding his extradition to their country to be tried for crimes against it.

The word *appeasement* is rarely used except in the context of Neville Chamberlain's deal with Hitler in 1938, but what about the present appeasement of Muslims in Britain?

It is obviously impossible to genuinely respect an ideology that our reason rejects as superstition, let alone *dangerous* superstition; so what the motion that we should respect it actually means is that we should *pretend* to respect religion for the sake of political correctness. Thus, at the very least, the motion that I was debating in Oxford demands hypocrisy.

But hypocrisy is not the worst of it.

When the ideologies that we pretend to respect are allowed to indoctrinate children, some of whom may even grow up to be suicide bombers because of it, hypocrisy becomes complicity in the mental abuse of children, the oppression of women, and even incitement to terrorism. This has been exacerbated by our political representatives, for the sake of votes, setting up state-supported schools to promote indoctrination in a particular faith, though they themselves probably accept a different, incompatible set of superstitions. We are told that Islam itself cannot be blamed for the terrorists' attacks on New York, Madrid, and London, followed by widespread carnage in retaliation for the publication of a few innocuous drawings. That is like saying that the horrors of the Inquisition had nothing to do with Christianity.

In the Gospels, Jesus consistently identifies righteousness with *believing* in him; and in the ages of faith the statement by Thomas Aquinas that "Unbelief is the greatest of sins" was incontrovertible. Hence, the Inquisition, the Crusades, and the Christian burning of witches, heretics, and Jews—the flames being fanned by Christian faith.

This use of torture was not a case of bad people perverting a good religion; the persecution of skeptics follows logically from the Christian correlation of faith with salvation, not to mention the scary notion that God could punish the whole of society for the disbelief of a few.

Muhammad followed on from Jesus, and the Qur'an contains even more manic denunciations of disbelief than the New Testament. Moreover, Islam has failed to moderate its cruel practices to the extent that mainstream Christianity has done in the past couple of centuries.

The Taliban, Al Qaeda, and Iraq's Badr Corps (commanded by that country's Supreme Council for Islamic Revolution) are certainly extremist, but they are orthodox—deriving logically from the Qur'an, which denigrates women and tells believers to wage *jihad* against heretics and infidels. Moderate Muslims may explain it away as misinterpretation—but why, then, did Allah or his Prophet lapse into ambiguity? Even the two major Islamic sects, Shia and Sunni, are at each other's throats in Iraq and elsewhere.

Muslims, we are told, are sensitive and are really hurt when their religion is joked about. Don't they credit their supposed creator god with any sense of humor? Didn't he actually invent laughter? And is he too weak to withstand a joke without some humorless cleric rushing to his defense? Or is their own faith so weak that they fear its contamination? Let them heed the old playground retort: "Sticks and stones may break my bones, but words can never hurt me."

Claiming to be ultrasensitive and really hurt by mere words or pictures is, of course, a way of gaining privilege. Everyone else has to speak softly so as not to hurt you.

It is argued that, since the common-law offense of blasphemy survives in Britain, though only for the protection of the doctrines of the Church of England, parity demands that the law be extended to protect other religions. But it is now practically a dead letter, and the best solution would clearly be to abolish it altogether, as, in fact, the Law Commission has recommended several times to succeeding governments, the ears of which are more deaf even than those of a person my age. But now the concept of blasphemy has been given an *independent* lease of life by renaming it "disrespect for religious feelings."

Our present government has even endeavored to criminalize such disrespect with another change of name, "incitement to religious hatred"; but, fortunately, ameliorating amendments to the relevant bill introduced in the House of Lords were finally accepted in the Commons—by just a single vote, when Blair himself was absent—on January 31 this year. But the attenuated bill then became law.

Of course, the law should protect *people*—in fact, that is basically what law is all about—and we have plenty of general laws for the protection of people, without special laws for the protection of *ideas* of a particular kind.

On February 20, Pope Benedict XVI called for mutual respect for all the world religions and their symbols—though he failed to mention, of course, parallel respect for atheism.

Anyway, how can the pope sincerely respect Islam when it teaches that believers in the "blasphemous" Christian Trinity are destined to spend eternity in hell? Not to mention that the death sentence is often passed in Muslim countries, to this day, on anyone who converts from Islam to Christianity.

The *fatwa* recently issued by Shia Grand Ayatollah Ali al-Sistani states not only that all homosexuals should be killed but that they should be killed in the "most severe way" possible. By comparison, Pope Benedict's homophobia is quite restrained.

Pressured by religious leaders sinking their differences in the common cause of authoritarianism, the Council of Europe is currently considering the introduction of legislation in the European Parliament and even the United Nations to enforce "respect for religious feelings" internationally.

Insertion of the word *feelings* lends this tendentious goal a semblance of humane empathy. But religion cannot, in all conscience, be intellectually respected if honesty is to prevail over hypocrisy—and giving it false respect would not just be obsequious and dishonest, but it would actually allow superstitions of the Dark Ages to triumph, destroying the whole range of social and individual freedoms courageously won over the past few centuries.

So, for the sake of liberty as well as truth, we must resist the indefensible furtherance of hypocritical respect. Far from being willing to moderate free speech by respect for religion, we should moderate respect for religion in favor of free speech.

Barbara Smoker was president of Britain's National Secular Society. She was recently honored with a lifetime achievement award for Distinguished Services to Humanism.

My God, How the Money Rolls In

James A. Haught

A jobless West Virginian, living on welfare, began preaching in Pentecostal tabernacles to support his family. Within a few years, T.D. Jakes had raked in so much money from believers that he was able to pay $870,000 for two side-by-side mansions, one with a pool and bowling alley. Then his soaring cash flow enabled him to pay $3.2 million for a Texas megachurch vacated by a crooked evangelist who had gone to prison. Before long, Jakes was grossing more than $20 million annually. Today, he ranks among America's flagrantly rich preachers, traveling by private jet, wearing enormous diamonds, living like royalty.

We've seen all this before, whether on an individual or institutional scale. Thirty-two centuries ago, during the reign of Ramses III, Egypt's great temple of the supreme god, Amun-Re—supposed creator of the world and father of the pharaoh—owned 420,000 head of livestock, sixty-five villages, eighty-three ships, 433 orchards, vast farmlands, and eighty-one thousand workers, all obeying the ruler priests. In medieval Europe, as the church acquired tighter control over all facets of life, the clergy discovered a gold mine: simony—the sale of blessings. Fees for absolution, baptism, burial, marriage, and the like escalated into a cash-and-carry system whose wares included the sale of high church offices. Most outrageous were indulgences, church documents bought by worried families to release dead relatives from the alleged pain of an invisible purgatory. In the 1200s, Pope Innocent III denounced simony, saying the clergy "are enthralled to avarice, love presents, and seek rewards; for the sake of bribes they pronounce the godless righteous."

In every age, in almost every culture, priestcraft has been a ticket to comfort. Churches and holy men reap earnings and exalted status from the supernaturalism they administer to their followers. As self-proclaimed emissaries of invisible spirits, they outrank the common folk who support them.

The Internal Revenue Service says Americans took tax exemptions for $88 billion in religious donations in 2004—thus the U.S. Treasury funded churches by forgoing taxes on that $88 billion. And this total doesn't count unknowable sums dropped into Sunday collection plates. Religion is lucrative.

In 1931, amid the misery of the Great Depression, novelist Theodore Dreiser accused the churches and clergy of sponging off people—calling them parasites and hypocrites railing against "sin" while doing little for the hungry. "For it is not men who are talking, as they assert, but God through them," Dreiser wrote in *Tragic America,* "and so through the mouths of tricksters and social prestidigitators, and no more and no less, comes all this hooey in regard to the hereafter." Two centuries earlier, in *The Age of Reason,* Thomas Paine likewise wrote that religions are "no other than human inventions, set up to terrify and enslave mankind, and monopolize power and profit."

Through the years, other writers have sounded similar warnings. Yet most people rarely think about the giant earnings accruing to faith or their consequences. The topic mostly escapes notice.

For example, how many know that riches from religion contributed to the downfall of classical Greece? Few have heard of the Sacred Wars that helped deliver the peninsula into the hands of Alexander the Great. Here's the historical account: in Ancient Greece, priests reaped wealth through various methods. One, apparently, was sacred prostitution. The Greek historian-philosopher-geographer Strabo wrote that Corinth's Aphrodite temple had one thousand consecrated women who served male worshipers for fees, enriching the temple. Presumably, the holy hookers were slave women, visited especially by sailors arriving at the large Corinth seaport. If Strabo's account is accurate, religion spawned a profitable bordello.

Even more lucrative were oracles, the fortune-tellers who captivated the ancient world. Superstitious Greeks flocked to oracles. First, the worshipers purified themselves by bathing and prayer, then they paid dearly to hear mumbo jumbo from priests and priestesses. At Dodona, a barefoot priestess sat on a high cliff, listening to the supposed voice of Zeus in the rustle of leaves or the flutter of dove wings. She provided yes-or-no answers to written questions. At Delphi (named for a dolphin that Apollo allegedly became), a stuporous priestess breathed vapors in a grotto and gave incoherent answers, which were then "translated" by a priest. The messages were murky—but swallowed avidly by paying believers.

As the fame of the Delphi shrine spread, so did its storehouse of gold, silver, and jewels taken from gullible clients. Kings and generals came to Delphi, seeking Apollo's guidance on important decisions, and they brought rich donations to the gods. Soon, various city-states built treasuries around the shrine to hold the wealth. The Amphictyonic League, a consortium of twelve city-states including Athens and Sparta, governed Delphi cooperatively and secured its riches, like directors of a bank.

But money breeds trouble. The Phocians, mountain people whose territories surrounded the shrine, saw an opportunity to cash in on the holy traffic and began levying steep fees on visitors. Other members of the league sent troops to halt the extra profiteering. The Phocians resisted. The First Sacred War erupted in 601 B.C.E. and lasted ten years. The Phocians were defeated and forced to serve the shrine.

A century later, in 480 B.C.E., a Persian army under Xerxes marched on Delphi to seize its wealth, but a landslide (caused by Apollo, the faithful said) blocked the troops.

A generation later, Phocians again grabbed Delphi's treasuries, and the Amphictyonic League again attacked. This Second Sacred War, in 447 B.C.E., ended like the first.

Seventy years after that, a different stash of religious wealth was looted. During many, many wars between Greek city-states, an Arcadian army plundered the treasuries of the mighty temple of Zeus at Olympia in southwest Greece. Naturally, this theft triggered more warring by kings and assemblies who had donated riches to the supreme god.

Soon afterward, back at Delphi, the Third Sacred War flared in 356 B.C.E., when the Phocians seized the Apollo shrine once more. Phocian leaders promised not to loot the treasuries—but soon did so. The wealth that had been drained from believers was squandered to hire mercenary soldiers to battle neighbors, to bribe opposing generals, and to reward cronies. Historian Charles Morris related:

> One hundred seventeen ingots of gold and 360 golden goblets went to the melting pot, and with them a golden statue three cubits high, and a lion of the same precious metal. And what added to the horror of pious Greece was that much of the pro-

ceeds of these treasures was lavished on favorites. Necklaces of Helen and Eriphyle were given to dissolute women, and a woman flute-player received a silver cup and a golden wreath from the temple hoard.

This time, the Amphictyonic League had been sadly weakened by centuries of fighting, especially by the Peloponnesian War between Athens and Sparta and by constant conflict with Persia. From the north, King Philip of Macedonia had been gaining power, expanding his territory, and sending legions in attempts to grab Greek lands. After the Delphi shrine was seized a third time, some local assemblies asked Philip to drive out the occupying Phocians. Shrewdly, he obliged. Posing as a devoted champion of Apollo, he waged a long war that finally quelled the temple grabbers. To inflict the vengeance of the god upon the looters, Philip drowned three thousand Phocian prisoners on charges of sacrilege. Subtly, he formed Greek "alliances" that made him *de facto* ruler and protector of the holies.

Then the Fourth Sacred War erupted in 339 B.C.E., after a different neighbor state invaded the sanctified Delphi region. The Amphictyonic League asked the Macedonian army to save the oracle temple again. However, some city-states perceived that Philip was using his defense of Apollo as a pretext to seize large sections of the peninsula. They fielded troops to resist—but ten thousand Macedonians in full battle array were unstoppable. At a crucial clash at Chaeronea, Philip's army crushed Athens, Thebes, and other allies. Philip's son, Alexander—who had been born at the start of the Third Sacred War—was a brilliant eighteen-year-old cavalry commander in the decisive massacre.

Victory in the Fourth Sacred War gave Philip complete control of Greece, except for defiant Sparta in the south. But he didn't live to rule. He was assassinated in 336 B.C.E., and Alexander took command. Greece was subsumed beneath Macedonia into a mighty war machine, Alexander's engine of conquest. The era of city-states ended. After Alexander's death, Greece fell under Roman rule. More than two thousand years were to pass before it regained independence.

Although ancient Greece saw multitudes of wars, and other self-destructive factors abounded, the wealth that priests took from the gullible was an important trigger that helped to topple the classical civilization. It's a little-known footnote in the age-old tale of riches from religion. Apparently, the tale never will end, as long as believers feel compelled to give tribute to purveyors of the supernatural.

James Haught is the editor of the Charleston (West Virginia) Gazette *and a senior editor at* Free Inquiry. *He is also the author of several books, including* Holy Hatred *(Prometheus Books 1994).*

AN EID TOO FAR

Christopher Hitchens

At the end of June, the New York City Council passed a nonbinding resolution that is sure to mark the beginning of a long and miserable dispute. The resolution called for the addition of two Muslim religious holidays to the number of days that the city's schoolchildren already get to take as vacation. To this recognition of Eid al-Fitr and Eid al-Adha, the mayor of New York, Michael Bloomberg, declared himself opposed. And by the nature of his opposition he, too, ensured that the future of this dispute will be poisonous. He said that school holidays should only be allowed for those religions that can boast "a very large number of kids who practice," and he added, "If you close the schools for every single holiday, there won't be any school."

Why do I say that it's obvious that this is a warning of crude times to come? First of all, because of what was said in support of the resolution by Imam Talib Abdur-Rashid, who is the head of the Mosque of Islamic Brotherhood in Harlem. "We really have confidence in the mayor's intelligence," said the imam, while warning that failure on Bloomberg's part to support the resolution could be "catastrophic." After all, he observed, "It's an election year."

If the imam thinks in this Tammany way, it's because he has

been taught to do so by Bloomberg himself. After all, the last time it was an election year in New York, Bloomberg managed to keep quiet about the disgusting scandal of rabbinical genital mutilation, where it was found that several children had been infected—at least one lethally—with genital herpes after a rabbi had insisted on practicing the ancient custom of placing the circumcised penis in his mouth. As this argument goes on, the mayor will find his own arguments being used against him: it will soon enough be proved that the Muslim religion can boast enough "kids who practice." As for preferring school time to religion time, it won't be long before it is openly said that in that case, Jewish holidays, or holy days, should not be observed either.

The latter point is one that should have been made by now in any case. I teach part-time at the New School for Social Research in New York, a university that was partly founded on hospitality and refuge for those forcibly exiled from Hitler's Germany. More than once while trying to schedule a class in the fall term, I have found that the whole school is closed on certain days because of some Mosaic or Abrahamic observance. Nobody has ever been able to explain to me why this should be the case in a secular institution open to students of all faiths and none. So I was pleased to see that one member of the city council—just one!—not only voted against the resolution but also accepted the logical consequence of his vote, which was to consider whether "the existing schedule of religious holidays might have to be reviewed and trimmed." (This was Councilman Oliver Koppell of the Bronx, in case you live in New York and want to support his reelection.)

We are reasonably lucky in the United States to have very few days wasted on officially sponsored holiday-making and, of those days, to have most of them derived from secular achievements. In spite of Ronald Reagan's crass attempt to argue that there should not be a special holiday for black Americans, most people think of Martin Luther King's birthday as a cause for general celebration. The same can be said, with a slight difference of emphasis, for Columbus Day. Thanksgiving has a spiritual undertone but is nonsectarian and devoted mainly to family. President's Day, Memorial Day, Independence Day, and Veterans' Day speak for themselves. And we are edging ever nearer to the point when Christmas/Hannukah/Kwanzaa has been sufficiently nationalized to be repackaged as the universal winter-solstice vacation with, as Thomas Jefferson used to say, "the compliments of the season."

Those who care enough about their own sect to take a day off school or work should be entitled to do so but should not require others, especially those of school age, to skip a day of education. *The New York Times* account of the debate managed to phrase it like this: "The holy days have long posed a painful choice for Muslim students: Should they go to class in the interests of their grades and attendance record, or cut class to be with their families?"

"Painful" I dare say it may be. But why should this be the taxpayers' problem? And why should the solution be the forced observance of the holy day by those who don't believe in its underlying tenets and don't even know what the day is supposed to signify? The article quoted an eighteen-year-old graduate of Stuyvesant High, Ms. Rebecca Chowdhury, who said that when young she had generally skipped school during the Eid holidays, but "as she grew older and faced more academic demands, she often had to forego the celebrations." I would say that she made the right choice and that it is the job of our education system to dissolve sectarian boundaries rather than to underline, emphasize, and indeed at least implicitly honor them. The calendar of such events needs to be pruned, not extended.

Christopher Hitchens is a columnist for Vanity Fair *and the author of* God Is Not Great *(Twelve Books), now out in paperback.*

THE SUBVERSION OF LISA BAUER

AN INTRODUCTION

Richard Dawkins

Religions puzzle me with their power to subvert otherwise intelligent minds and turn them in directions that an outside observer (and under normal circumstances, the subverted mind itself) would instantly recognize as ridiculous. Francis Collins is an excellent scientist whose success in running the huge organization that was the official American Human Genome Project demonstrates his cogent grasp of how the real world works. Suppose, now, that a candidate for an important and responsible job in Collins's organization announced at his interview that he liked to put a sprig of mistletoe in his hair and dance around a fairy ring in order to appease the forest sprites. Collins would immediately show him the door with a polite "Don't call us" and turn hastily to the next candidate. Yet what Collins himself believes—virgin mothers and the risen Jesus and frozen Trinitarian waterfalls—is just as thoroughly divorced from reality and sense. The point is that Collins himself would recognize this clearly but for the subversive power of religion.

That power to impose ridiculous beliefs on otherwise intelligent and sensible people is a fascinating phenomenon. It is vitally important that we understand it, but it's hard for us to appreciate its full weirdness when we live in a culture where the ridiculous beliefs concerned are deeply embedded. In America, Christianity and Judaism are so ubiquitous and familiar that we tend to overlook absurdities that an objective observer—the proverbial Martian, say—would have no trouble spotting. Similarly, it is hard for citizens of Iran or Afghanistan to notice the absurdities of Islam; it is too familiar, part of the default background of their culture.

It is, therefore, especially interesting when we encounter somebody of high intelligence who has voluntarily, sincerely, and over a long period embraced a faith that is alien to the culture in which she was brought up and has now recovered from it. Lisa Bauer is such a person. She was raised in an ordinary American home with no Muslim connections; she did well at an ordinary American university; and yet she voluntarily, and apparently without coercion (that came later) embraced Islam. This was no passing whim: she did the thing properly, with the utmost sincerity and seriousness, and she stuck with it for seven years before eventually seeing the light and becoming an atheist.

It was toward the end of her Islamic period that I first became aware of Lisa. She wrote me an e-mail that began *"Asalaamu alaikum* (Peace be upon you) Professor Dawkins" and continued with what sounded to me pretty much like a cry for help:

> I desperately wish I could make up my mind about what it is I believe. Although I pray five times a day, I am assaulted at least fifty times a day by the thought that there is no Allah, no God at all, and that all the praying and fasting for Ramadan and reciting the Qur'an (in Arabic, of course) that I do is for nothing.

The letter was signed with an Arabic name, so I complimented her on her excellent English, which I said would put most British and American native speakers to shame. She then told me her native language was indeed English. She was an American convert to Islam.

Not wishing to exert an undue influence on somebody so evidently vulnerable, I responded to her cry for help by sending her a couple of books (by Ibn Warraq and Ayaan Hirsi Ali), although I later learned that there was almost nothing she hadn't read. I also suggested that she might find friendship and support on the forums of RichardDawkins.net. She did so, and she soon began to fill the role—highly necessary—of unofficial fact-checker, developing a reputation among our regulars for scrupulous accuracy and knowledge (a reputation that she more than lived up to when I later employed her to check facts and prepare the bibliography of my new book, *The Greatest Show on Earth*). I like to think that the sympathy and good fellowship she encountered on our forums may have encouraged her to escape the clutches of Islam.

Her seven years as a Muslim had an effect on Lisa (as she again calls herself) and her psychology that could fairly be described as a personal disaster, and she is only now recovering, with help. I suggested that she write an account of her experience, perhaps eventually at book length but, as a first step, as a series of three articles in *Free Inquiry*. Fortunately, she is not only intelligent and well-read, she is also a very good writer, with the ability to express herself and explain what it felt like, from the inside, to be taken over, body and mind, by a ludicrous and pernicious belief system: taken over so thoroughly that she even . . . but let her tell her own story.

Richard Dawkins, a renowned evolutionary biologist and activist for public understanding of science, is senior editor and columnist for Free Inquiry. *His latest book is* The Greatest Show on Earth *(Ballantine, 2009).*

SUBJECTION AND ESCAPE
PART 1
AN AMERICAN WOMAN'S MUSLIM JOURNEY
Lisa Bauer

On Monday, the eleventh of February, 2002, I apprehensively stepped through the doors of the local mosque to recite the profession of faith that would make me a Muslim. I was a very shy, naïve, young American woman with absolutely no direct personal experience of Islam, and I had no idea about what to expect. Even though this was a mosque located in the heart of a good-sized American city, it still seemed a foreign, mysterious place to me. Would the people there be kind and accepting or mysterious and forbidding? I took a seat in the foyer to await the arrival of the imam of the mosque and looked around, my head awkwardly covered with a thin black scarf I'd bought a few days before. There were only a handful of men in the building, waiting for the noon prayer.

Where was the imam, anyway? We had spoken on the telephone the day before, when I'd summoned the courage to finally call the mosque to say that I wanted to convert to Islam. When? Today, if possible! Well, it was Sunday, and that would make things difficult. I finally agreed to come to the mosque the next day, Monday, and the imam told me that he would meet me then so I could make my *shahadah*, the testimony of faith. I'd been practicing the Arabic words for a couple of days and was fairly confident that I could recite them when asked. Now all I needed were the two or more Muslim witnesses whose presence would make it official.

The next morning, I took the bus to the mosque, a small, domed building located right next to the university. I'd passed by it a few times before but had never had the courage to step inside. That was why I'd telephoned first, because I wanted to get some more information before daring to enter such an unfamiliar place. It was much less forbidding once I'd made my appointment, but I still opened those doors with my heart in my throat, nervous and terrified that I'd breach some rule or custom.

That wasn't long in coming. After waiting around nervously for a little while, I took off my shoes, left them in the space provided, and entered the prayer room, just to have a look around. There was an expanse of blue carpet covering the floor, with permanent depressions to mark out lines for prayer. The walls were whitewashed and unadorned, and in front there was a closed, roll-away room divider—the room could be expanded into the main prayer area for Friday prayer, but at the time I didn't know what was behind it. There was a small door in the back left corner, with a smaller prayer room visible. I picked a line in the main room and began to go through the motions of the Muslim prayer ritual, which I had been practicing for some weeks, using index cards to help me memorize the Arabic words. After I finished, I noticed a man behind me who told me a bit apologetically that this was actually the men's prayer room! The smaller one was for women. I apologized and left the room, deeply ashamed.

The imam finally arrived, and I gratefully stood to greet him. We went into his office and spoke for a little while about how I'd found Islam and what I would have to do to make my *shahadah*. A Jordanian Arab, he had only been in America for a couple of years;

he spoke English with a very heavy accent. He was friendly and very interested in me, which put me at ease.

When we finished speaking, he took me to the main prayer room. There was an Islamic elementary school on the premises, and at this point a class of children, perhaps seven or eight years of age, were sitting in there with their teacher, a young woman in an *abaya* (black overgarment) I'll call Noor. The imam had me go up to the microphone and repeat what he said to me.

"*Ash-hadu anna la illaha illallah, wa ash-hadu anna Muhammad ur-rasul Allah.* I bear witness that there is no god but Allah, and I bear witness that Muhammad is his messenger."

"*Takbir!*" the imam commanded, smiling, and all the children yelled "*Allahu Akbar!*" ("God is great") as one. "*Takbir!*" he said again, and the children repeated their cry. The imam said "*Takbir!*" a third time, the children once again cried out that God is great, and then Noor hugged me. Afterward, the imam and I returned to his office, and I asked for a certificate of conversion, since I had fantasies of making the *hajj,* and the Saudi government won't let you get anywhere near Mecca without proof that you're a Muslim. The time for the noon prayer arrived shortly thereafter, and I felt my heart leap with joy and excitement when I finally heard the *adhan*, the call to prayer, being recited for the first time over the mosque loudspeaker system. I prayed with Noor in the women's section, and she offered to help me out as I was such a new Muslim. For most of the rest of the afternoon, I stayed at the mosque, speaking with Noor and the imam and asking questions. I had to leave around 2 P.M. for a class at the university, but after that I returned and spent some more time talking with them. Noor, I soon learned, was a convert like me, and she wore a *niqab*, a face veil, in public, which I was later to learn was very unusual in this community; all the other women I met at the mosque just wore the *hijab,* merely covering the hair. She seemed a very interesting and intriguing person, and I looked forward to getting to know her better.

How had I gotten myself into this situation? It's a long story. Five months earlier to the day, I'd watched on television, horrified, as the second of the World Trade Center towers collapsed. The night before, I hadn't been able to sleep until 5 A.M., and I was awakened a few hours later by my father telling me that the World Trade Center was on fire and that one of the towers had already collapsed. For the rest of the day, I sat in something of a daze, glued to the television, unable to make any sense of what was going on.

There was a personal side to the tragedy. Two years previously, I'd dragged my mother and younger sister with me to visit New York City, the first time for any of us, because I so desperately wanted to go there. While we were there, we'd visited the Twin Towers, and I still had my $12.50 adult admission ticket stub. Thinking of that, I dug out all my New York souvenirs, finally found the stub, and looked at it despondently.

It really hit me hard. After all, I'd actually *been* in those buildings; the World Trade Center wasn't just some meaningless name to me. I remembered the huge entrance lobby, the superfast visitor's elevator, and the visitor's center on the top floor of the second tower, surrounded by huge windows where people could look out at the skyline. There was a restaurant, several gift shops, a small theater that took you on a "ride" over the city, even making the seats move along with the action on the screen. Tucked in a corner was a scale model of the city. All gone. I remembered the bank of telephones where I'd called a friend I'd met in the city while we were there. I also remembered how angry my mother had been because the observation deck on the roof was closed due to ice. It was March and still winter, and New York had just had a snowfall! Gone, all gone—maybe along with some of the people I'd happened to see there, too.

The terrible events of September 11, 2001, had a rather strange effect on me. Instead of provoking intense rage or bitter hatred, they served to spark an intense curiosity in me about Islam. What was it about Islam and the Muslim world that had led people to do these things? I had been interested in the Middle East ever since I was a child and had learned about the great ancient civilizations of the region. I had also taken a couple of classes on the subject when I was a student at the university. In fact, I'd even purchased an English translation of the Qur'an, the one by M.H. Shakir, which I'd chosen because it was the only translation at the bookstore in which each individual verse was numbered instead of only every fifth verse. I had even read it all the way through, having decided that I could not call myself educated if I didn't know what was in the holy text of Islam. I'd already read the Bible through at least three times, so that wasn't an especially unusual whim for me. Still, as it had been a few years, I simply couldn't recall much of what I'd read. I dug out the small paperback volume and proceeded to reread it. However, I wasn't sure what to make of much of the text, since there were no notes and the Qur'an is written in a rather elliptical style that alludes to events more than it spells them out.

No, I needed a new translation, one that I recalled reading a bit at the university library some time ago. It had been a really nice, green, hardcover volume with the Arabic text and English translation in parallel columns, and best of all, it had notes. I wanted one for myself. I searched the bookstores, but frustratingly I couldn't find anything like it. My next stop was Amazon.com (I wasn't used to purchasing books online at the time), and there it was—Abdullah Yusuf Ali's *The Meaning of the Holy Qur'an*. I quickly bought a copy and added to my order a few other introductory books about Islam. When they finally arrived I devoured them all.

There was something about the Qur'an and Islam that fascinated me, something I still can't fully explain. I just couldn't get enough of the subject. I began to visit Islamic Web sites in an effort to find out more about the religion and even worked up the courage to send in a question to an Islamic Q&A *fatwa* site. (A *fatwa* is simply an opinion about some aspect of Islamic law issued by a Muslim scholar and does not actually mean a death sentence, contrary to Western perceptions after the Salman Rushdie affair.) I got a quick reply from a young Egyptian man—a *hafiz*, meaning that he had memorized the entire Qur'an—and we began exchanging e-mails on a regular basis. I asked him about various aspects of the religion, and he answered my questions very patiently. I wasn't always convinced by what he was saying, but at least I was communicating with a bona fide Muslim! I didn't know any Muslims personally at the time—admittedly, my social circle was extremely limited—and so I was really pleased to be in contact with such a knowledgeable representative of Islam.

I was also obsessed with learning more about not just the religion of Islam but also anything associated with the Islamic world. I plowed through quite a few volumes concerning the finer points of Islam, the history of the Islamic world, Islamic art and architecture, even tangential matters such as the pre-Islamic history of the region. All cultures and people that had some connection with Islam were fair game—Arabs, Iranians, Turks, Africans, Indians, Pakistanis—anybody at all.

I lost count of the number of hours I spent staring at

photographs of the exquisite art and architecture of the Islamic world, and I ended up being simply smitten. Something about the culture and the art, as well as the religion, touched me very deeply, and the more I studied and the more books I read, the more I wanted to not just study it but become a part of it, somehow. When I contemplated the blue tiling and graceful calligraphy of the *Masjid-i Shah* (Royal Mosque), now known as the *Masjid-i Imam* (Mosque of the Imam), in Isfahan, Iran, for example, I couldn't shake the feeling that to truly be able to fully appreciate it, I would need to accept the religion that inspired it. Of course, it's perfectly possible for somebody to appreciate a work of religious art without subscribing to the underlying belief system, but it seemed to me that the full effect could really only be experienced by a believer. A nonbeliever can admire a cathedral or stained-glass representations of biblical stories or Bach's *St. Matthew Passion*, but in such cases the appreciation may be somewhat distant or detached. You're admiring the art and maybe have a vague sense of the artistic spirit that sparked it, but as for the specifically religious content of the work, well . . . it may not really move you since you don't believe in it. If you are a believer, though, your appreciation has considerably more depth—Bach isn't just setting some silly old fable to music; he's retelling the story of the pivotal event in human history. Similarly, a non-Muslim may well be able to appreciate the beautiful decoration and calligraphy of the Taj Mahal, but to a Muslim, the eighty-three verses of *surah Ya Seen* from the Qur'an (a chapter commonly recited for the dead), twisting their way around the four portals in elegant calligraphy, can be especially moving in context, since the structure was built as a tomb for the wife of the Mughal emperor Shah Jahan.

After I converted, or "reverted" in Islamic parlance (as all children are said by Islam to be born Muslim and converts are just "reverting" to their original religion), I continued to devour books and any other source of information about what was now "my" *ummah*, the "nation" of all Muslims, my "brothers" and "sisters" in Islam. No book was too detailed or specialized for me. I read anthropological and sociological studies of Moroccan *madrasa*s, memoirs of secular Iranian women struggling to break free from that country's theocracy, treatises on the finer architectural details of mosques and minarets, and so on. I even delved into dissenting views, such as Ibn Warraq's books, since I wanted to get as many perspectives as possible. I'm sure many of those who read *Not Without My Daughter* or saw the film were horrified at how the author and her daughter were trapped in Iran by her tyrannical husband. By contrast, I was very intrigued and even moved by the author's depiction of everyday life in Tehran, even though the book and film have been widely excoriated as presenting a grossly unfair depiction of Iranian society and reinforcing damaging stereotypes of Muslims. To me, all voices had to be considered, since they all possessed some truth.

Such were my intellectual obsessions. But, you may ask, what was my emotional state? I've said much about the intellectual roots of my embrace of Islam; how was I *feeling*? What made me open to the notion of completely changing my life by embracing a whole new religion?

I was really adrift at that point in my life. I had completed my university degree in creative writing but had not found a job, and I wasn't sure what to do next. I'd signed up for some courses at the local community college in hopes of getting a certificate or degree in a subject more immediately salable in the job market than creative writing, probably something having to do with computers. I'm not sure why I never considered going on to graduate school; I think I'd more or less had enough of formal education, which I had found stultifying and dull. I was actually quite ashamed of myself for being what I thought was a failure, since I had very little income, and at the time I was living in my parents' house as I couldn't afford to live anywhere else. I had money for books, but that was only because I had money left over from my student loan.

I was also extremely lonely—as usual. All my life, I've been very quiet and shy; making friends has always been an exceptionally difficult challenge for me. Speaking with other people was a real struggle, too, and I developed a fear and mistrust of other people that proved devastating for my social life and my self-confidence. In addition, I felt that I had very little in common with my peers, who were generally engaged in typical adolescent activities like gossiping or shopping for clothes while I preferred to spend my free time prowling the stacks at the library or studying the encyclopedia. School had been no help for me in that regard. I had decided from an early age that school had nothing to do with education or learning; I associated it with having to repeat and relearn things I already knew. My family, while kind and loving, didn't share my overriding passion for acquiring knowledge (or should I say facts?), so I couldn't really talk to them about a lot of the things most important to me. When I began learning about Islam, I didn't feel I could share any of my newfound passion with them. They knew I was buying books about the subject, but they thought that was just another one of my periodic intellectual obsessions—and I didn't say or do anything to make them think differently.

It's a bit strange that I have gotten this far in my story, ostensibly about my embrace of a particular religion, without mentioning what I actually believed. I don't think I honestly *believed* in any kind of supernatural beings or religions at the time my obsession began. I certainly hadn't been looking for any groups or experiences of a specifically spiritual or religious nature.

The first thoughts I clearly remember having about religion and God, when I was a small child of perhaps six or seven, were that the entire concept of God was stupid and that religion was obvious garbage. I don't know how I had arrived at that conclusion; it surely hadn't come from my parents! I loved reading about science as a child, especially astronomy, and that probably had something to do with it. I was a fairly hard-core atheist, at least as much as a child can be, but I remember being troubled when I contemplated the idea of my own death. My child's brain wondered if I would see blackness, like when I closed my eyes, or whether death would be like sleeping. Finally, I decided that I would be as I had been before I was born, and I realized that I would see nothing at all. Not that these ruminations made me happy, mind you. As I got a little older, I would sometimes have panic attacks when I thought about death and the idea that there would be simply nothing afterward. Those were never pleasant experiences! I remember being upset that nobody in my family seemed to have any understanding of my fears, though perhaps that was just childish egoism.

For reasons that remain murky to me, when I was eleven, my parents decided that now was the time to finally try to give my younger siblings and me some kind of religious education. Up until then, there had been essentially nothing along those lines, even though we had all been baptized Roman Catholic. My experience with religion had been confined to a few Christmas and Easter services, to which I paid little attention. But now they started taking us to a nearby Catholic church every week. (I admit that I hesitated a bit about naming the denomination here, because I'm actually ashamed that I ever had any association with that foul, disgusting organization. Then again, I suppose it can't be any worse than voluntarily converting to Islam!)

It was actually rather odd because my mother disliked much about the Church. She'd been sent to a Catholic school as a child and had had some *extremely* negative experiences there, with the nuns verbally abusing her and treating her like garbage. She loathed the sexism inherent in the patriarchal structure and the rules of the Church. I suppose that she and my father wanted to give us children some religious exposure, and it was the only church they knew. (Later on, she would shuck off Catholicism and start attending more liberal churches of other denominations, at least for a short while.)

My reaction to all of this was not what might have been expected. Up until then, as I've mentioned, I'd thought religion was a lot of rubbish and that the very idea of God was ridiculous. But now, for some reason, I became deeply interested in religion. As I've already said, I'm not sure how much of it I actually believed, but I wanted to know all about it. I remember feeling uneasy when I looked through my junior edition encyclopedia, not having the slightest idea who these people Moses and Joshua and David and so on were. We didn't even have a Bible in the house, and I knew absolutely nothing about what it contained. So in a way this opened a whole new intellectual horizon for me.

I remember being put into weekly CCD (Confraternity of Christian Doctrine—religious education) classes at the church and quickly becoming bored, because they didn't impart enough factual information about the Bible or the Church for my taste!

I asked for and received a really nice Bible as a gift for my first, belated Communion when I was twelve, which I read cover to cover. (Supposedly this is a really unusual thing for Catholics to do, given their stereotypically weak knowledge of the Bible.) I became somewhat annoyed with the Church's relative lack of emphasis on the Bible in favor of various Catholic teachings. A teacher told me in a CCD class that the Church was based on "the Bible and tradition," though it seemed to me that the latter far overshadowed the former.

No doubt one of the reasons that I found the Bible so appealing was because it was, after all, a work of ancient history, and I loved ancient history. I'm not sure how much I actually believed what I was reading; it was more that I was drawn in by the sheer historical sweep of the narrative. The Old Testament seemed far more interesting to me than the New because it dealt with a much longer span of time and seemed more ancient. I also liked reading about the history of the Church and the saints, since I loved reading history and biographies so much. I recall developing a disparaging view of certain Protestant "born-again" churches because they had no apparent sense of history. Some people seemed to think that Christianity today, the way they practiced it in their churches, was exactly the way it had been in the time of the apostles, and they took the Bible absolutely literally. They were the kind of Christians who proverbially say, "If English was good enough for Jesus, it's good enough for me!"

Still, the entire time that I was supposedly a model Catholic girl, I was tormented by doubts about the whole enterprise. It wasn't points like whether Jesus was really born of a virgin that bothered me, as those seemed secondary and rather unimportant, but the more fundamental question of the very existence of God. I just couldn't fully accept the idea. I attributed this to my long years of disbelief. I envied the way my mother, for example, seemed to naturally accept the existence of God even if she rejected most of the rest of what the Church taught. Perhaps, I remember thinking, a bit bitterly, I would have had that faith, too, had I been brought up from earliest childhood to believe in God.

But now I'm not so sure; after my experiences, I'm more inclined to believe that some people are instinctively less inclined to such belief than others, and so religion won't really "take" with them. Witness what happened a few years later.

My interest in religion waned some time in high school, after I'd been confirmed, and my family gradually stopped going to church. I should note that I never felt at any time that religion was being shoved down my throat. Sure, I was being taken to church, but on some level, I always thought of religion as something I could take or leave. I can't say I ever feared hell or even really believed in it, and I can honestly state that the infamous Catholic guilt was never a part of my experience. Although I did think that it was important to try to follow the dictates of the Church, for example, not eating meat on Fridays during Lent, I didn't feel that any such practice was forcibly imposed on me. In fact, *I* tended to be the one who scrupulously tried to follow the rules, while my parents and siblings more or less ignored them. I never bothered them about that, though, because I never thought it was my place to tell others how to live. No, I would follow the rules because I (sort of) believed in them, not because anybody was forcing me, and if I ceased to believe, I would stop.

And that's basically what I did. I stopped midway through high school and more or less reverted to my "natural state" of atheism. Well, not quite! Although I didn't really believe in anything supernatural anymore, I had this new sense that I really didn't know for sure and so shouldn't be as quick as I had been to dismiss the whole notion, a weak sort of agnosticism. I certainly wasn't as militant as I had been. I understood more about religion now and was far more patient with it. In fact, I would get irritated when I read articles or books by people who seemed to have no understanding whatever of religion and what it meant to its followers and made no effort to see where religious people were coming from, preferring to deal in crude stereotypes of what they thought religious people believed instead of treating them as actual people with complex internal lives. Religion was an important subject that needed to be understood, not just blithely dismissed, I thought. Still, I was very sympathetic to skepticism. While a university student, I remember spending long hours in the university library going through back copies of *Skeptical Inquirer* and similar periodicals and reading books like Carl Sagan's *The Demon-Haunted World*.

This state of affairs, in which I didn't think much about the existence of God or the truth of religion, continued until I became interested in Islam. There was a brief period when I was interested in the historical and cultural roots of Judaism, and I went on quite a reading spree about that, but I didn't feel that I could actually believe in it as a religion. Sure, when I read about the long and fascinating history of Judaism, I occasionally wished I could be part of that tradition; but there was no way I could accept all those rules in *halakha* (Jewish law)! This interest paved the way for my interest in Islam, however, in that many of the concepts and ideas found in (Orthodox and historical) Judaism, such as the emphasis on sacred law and the importance of orthopraxy (correct behavior), are also found in Islam. Over the years, I've come to realize just how strikingly similar the two religions are, which makes it all the more perplexing why there would be so much hatred between them. Or maybe it's not such a mystery. The fiercest battles seem to be between those who agree on the basics but differ regarding certain particulars—witness the bitter fights between slightly differing branches of Christianity, or between Sunnis and Shi'ites!

So now we come back to Islam. I want to go into more detail about what I found appealing about it, since that seems to be a major stumbling block whenever anybody hears my story—"Why on Earth *Islam*, of all things?!" I've been trying to show just how much of my initial burst of interest in Islam was not really based on the truth claims or beliefs of the religion but on everything else associated with it—its history, the different Muslim cultures and civilizations, and so on. If I'd been in a different state of mind or had had different inclinations about how best to appreciate Islam, I might have been happy to simply be another non-Muslim student of the Islamic world or the Middle East. Near East or Middle East studies departments in Western universities are filled with such people. There is something about the subject area that attracts certain people to it; there is a rich history of Westerners smitten, for lack of a better word, by the Islamic world. Examples include T.E. Lawrence (Lawrence of Arabia); Gertrude Bell, who with Lawrence created the modern state of Iraq; Sir Richard Burton, who wrote about making the *hajj* in disguise; St. John Philby, an aristocratic convert; Lady Evelyn Cobbold, the first British-born woman to make the *hajj*; and many others. Not all converted to Islam, of course, but they were certainly drawn in by the "mystique" of the region and religion, much as I was drawn into it.

But detached scholarly study wasn't good enough for me. No, as I mentioned before, I wanted to actually be part of Islam, not just be a student looking in. There was also something in the

Qur'an that appealed to me and made me consider that perhaps what it said really was true. Of course, now that sounds absolutely ridiculous, but I was very taken by it. Each time I read the Qur'an, I would try to suspend disbelief and accept it on its own terms, just to better experience what it might be like to be Muslim. And the more I engaged in such nonjudgmental reading, the more the beliefs of Islam began to seep into my brain and become more "reasonable." I suppose you could say I was indoctrinating myself through repetition.

By the time I finally converted, I'd gone through the Qur'an three times, and each time I accepted more and more of what it said. Nevertheless, there were some beliefs and rules that I didn't particularly care for and couldn't really make myself actively believe in. My response was twofold: first, I decided that if I couldn't really accept something like the actual, physical presence of two angels on my right and left sides, taking down my deeds (as the Qur'an teaches), I could at least passively accept the notion by not actively rejecting it. God, or Allah (and here I stifled my doubts about the existence of such a being) would know my intentions, right? He'd know that my heart was in the right place.

Second, during my initial study, I'd constructed a sort of liberal Islam for myself, one that didn't take the graphic depictions of the tortures of hellfire in the Qur'an literally. *Ar-Rahman*, the Most Merciful, wouldn't really torture people forever; didn't the Qur'an say that people would stay in hell "as long as Allah wills"? There was nothing preventing Allah from willing everybody to eventually end up in paradise, right? Those infamous verses about women were meant to be read in the context of their time, I thought. I'd discovered some Islamic feminist writers who used the Qur'an to argue for women's rights and the equality of the sexes, and I thought it wasn't impossible to reconcile at least some form of feminism with Islam.

Let's go back to the beginning, because there is a far darker aspect to this story. The day I became a Muslim, I spoke for quite a while to the imam who had converted me, discussing Islam, my life situation, and other subjects. He was a tall and rather heavy man, originally from Jordan, and he seemed quite genuinely interested in me. Along with writing me a certificate of conversion that first day, he also gave me a check for a hundred and fifty dollars (as I recall), since I'd mentioned how broke I was. I stayed until after the evening prayer, when he offered to take me home in his car. I accepted gratefully; it seemed a lot better than taking the bus and walking home in the dark. We spoke some more about my life and the possible problems I might have with my family over my conversion, and he dropped me off about a block from where I lived so that they wouldn't see him.

The next day, I returned to the mosque, and he and I were able to talk a little more. He seemed to really like me, I thought; he was always happy to listen to my problems and give advice. Noor, the young *niqab*-wearing woman, was also friendly and helpful to me. We discussed all sorts of things, and she even took me shopping for some new, more modest clothes, since my wardrobe consisted mostly of shorts and short-sleeved shirts, which just wouldn't do for a Muslim woman. The imam took me home again that night, picking me up at a bus stop some distance away from the mosque so that nobody would see us together, I supposed. I remember he told me at some point during the drive home, "You need someone to take care of you." I didn't disagree.

This continued for the rest of that week—I would spend much

of the day at the mosque, occasionally punctuated by my classes at the community college, and speak with the imam and Noor about what was going on, about Islam, and so on. He drove me home a couple more times, and one time I distinctly remember him kissing my hand as I left. I also remember sometime that week, while I was at the mosque, I became overwhelmed with feelings of depression and began to cry, and the imam took me into his office and talked to me for a little while. Then he suggested we go for a drive. I agreed.

We went to an empty house that the mosque owned, which was located on a large lot at some distance from the main road. The mosque was planning to use the land for a school at some point in the future, and that's why the imam had the keys to the place. We got out of the car and walked around the yard for a while, speaking together a little bit, before getting back in the car and heading back to the mosque. On some semiconscious level, it occurred to me that perhaps it wasn't such a good idea to be going to a deserted location with a man I didn't know very well, one so much older than I was, but I was hopelessly naïve. I may have been twenty-four years old, yet emotionally I felt eighteen, perhaps younger. This man was a respected imam, after all—what could I fear from him? He had a wife and three children, all of whom I'd met or at least seen, and they seemed to be a very nice, happy family.

We visited the house again the next day—I'm not sure why— and this time things were different. I remember sitting on the carpet in the empty living room with him and listening to him as he told me about the problems he was having. Since he was so eager to help me, I told him a little bit more about my own problems; we stood up to go, and he began to hug me. As he held me tightly, I could feel the unmistakable hardness of his erection against my thigh. He kissed me and asked me how I played with myself. I couldn't answer; I was simultaneously frightened to death and, strangely, a bit excited. He asked me if I wanted to see "it," and when I didn't say no, he took me into one of the bedrooms off the main hall, sat down, unzipped his fly, and began masturbating furiously. I don't know why I didn't run. Instead, I sat there watching, fascinated and disgusted at the same time, and when he finished we left.

I have no idea what the hell was going through my mind the next day, because I not only returned to the mosque, I also went back to the house with the imam and let him touch my body any way he wanted. I think I wanted to know what "it" was like. I'd never been with a man before and was insatiably curious about everything to do with sex. I was also very lonely, and the fact that this man was actually taking an interest in me seemed too good to be true. I do remember feeling awful about the fact that he was married and that all of this was completely forbidden under Islam, but I just couldn't seem to stop myself. I wasn't thinking rationally; I was probably just so desperate for somebody to care about me and talk to me that I threw all my inhibitions and morals out the window, even though this meant transgressing everything my newfound faith taught.

We fell into the habit of going out to the house almost every day during the afternoon, and these visits became more and more intense. We would engage in various forms of feverish foreplay before having to go back to the mosque an hour or two later, in time for the sunset prayer. Anything was fair game, other than actual vaginal intercourse. This way, I realized later, the imam could avoid the guilt of actually committing adultery, while getting as much as possible out of my "favors."

This was, as we both knew implicitly, an untenable state of affairs. Something would have to give. Fortunately for the imam, he had the perfect "Islamically acceptable" solution in mind, and it wouldn't take him long to put it into effect. It was a decision that I would come to regret enormously, but as it turned out, it was only the beginning of my destructive experience with Islam. Things were about to take a new and queasy turn, one that would lead me to the depths of despair, agony, and humiliation before I finally found the way out to physical and mental freedom.

Lisa Bauer is currently a graduate student and an aspiring writer. She is attempting to pick up the pieces of her life after her traumatic experience without the help or hindrance of any kind of religion.

SUBJECTION AND ESCAPE
PART 2
AN AMERICAN WOMAN'S
MUSLIM JOURNEY
Lisa Bauer

The alarm clock awakens me with its annoying buzz. Half-consciously, I smash down the snooze button. I peep out at the time: 5:32 A.M. I really must get up and shower. Then I can do my *wudu'* (ritual ablutions) and pray before the time for *fajr* (the dawn prayer) expires at sunrise, which according to my prayer-times chart is a few minutes past six. As the year progresses, the time for *fajr* gets ever earlier; after the longest day of the year, it reverses course and begins coming ever later. You can't just assume you know the time for prayer because you know what it was yesterday.

I roll out of bed and stamp off to the shower. I should be grateful, I remind myself. Allah has seen fit to grant me a job. I'm living in America, not the slums of Dhaka in Bangladesh. I have a car. My parents and siblings are still alive. I'm healthy. Well, maybe I have some problems, since I've been struggling with depression and I'm so incredibly shy, but at least I'm not crippled.

Not crippled? This shyness, timidity, whatever it is, has been as crippling to me in my life as having an arm or a leg cut off, I think bitterly as I begin shampooing my hair. Why has Allah made me thus? Why must I suffer so?

No, that's not the right way to think about it. Perhaps there is a reason for it all, one that will become clear as time goes on. Allah has His reasons—at least I hope He does. I wish I had more faith that He knows what He's doing, but I have a lot of doubts. And I should be careful about thinking I'm better off than people in the slums of Dhaka, because I don't know that either. Perhaps some of them are happier and more content than I am—only Allah knows.

I rinse off. Having completed *ghusl* (bathing that removes major ritual impurity), I should be pure enough to pray.

No such luck. Now I have to pee. Urination, along with defecation, flatulence, and bleeding, are causes of minor ritual impurity and require *wudu'* before you can pray. So does sleeping. Sex, menstruation, and sexual discharge, male or female, render one *junub* (having major ritual impurity) and require *ghusl*.

I sigh. I put on my robe and head to the sink. I turn on the water, murmur *"Bismillah"* ("In the name of Allah"), and begin rubbing my hands under the water. It's quite complicated. You have to wash your hands up to the wrists three times, starting with the right hand. Then you wash the mouth three times by gulping a little water, rinsing a bit, and then spitting out the water. Then you clean the nose by putting a bit of water into the nostrils and blowing it out, three times. Then you wash the face from the hairline to the chin and all the way to the ears, three times. And then you wash your arms, from the wrists to the elbow, starting with the right arm, three times. Then you wipe your head with wet hands, from the front to the back, and then wipe your ears—this is done only once. Finally, you wash your feet up to the ankles, starting with the right foot.

That's the tricky part. The first actions are straightforward and can be performed in rapid succession. But I have to put my feet in the sink in order to clean them, which can be daunting. I'm fairly limber, but I've heard stories of people slipping and falling as they are trying to clean their feet in the sink while doing *wudu'*. This is why it's better to have a foot bath like they have at the mosque—or use the bathtub, if you have one. (The toilet is considered "filthy" and cannot be used, if you're wondering.) Also, it's messy. The first steps of *wudu'* can be done with minimal water, but once I start washing my feet, I tend to get water all over the place.

My *wudu'* complete, I go back to my bedroom and dress myself in my usual loose black slacks, loose blouse, and a pair of black socks. I cover my hair with a two-piece Al Amirah *hijab*, a style popular among young people because it's easy to put on—no pins or intricate wrapping to deal with. Also, I like it because it is very effective at hiding every last strand of hair, which elastic holds in place around your head.

I step over to the horrible blue shag rug that I have set up as a prayer mat in a corner of the bedroom. My floor is tile, not carpet, and a regular prayer rug was not comfortable, especially when I put my forehead to the ground in *sujood* (prostration). So after considering the available choices, I bought a thick shag rug, about four feet by three feet. Nothing says you can't use any clean piece of cloth as a prayer mat; I'd used a towel in the early days.

I step onto the rug, facing northeast, the *qibla* (direction to Mecca). I take a deep breath, lower my eyes to the edge of the rug, and raise my hands to my ears, palms facing outward. *"Allahu akbar"* ("Allah is great"), I murmur softly. I fold my arms in front of me, the right hand grasping the left wrist, and start reciting the familiar Arabic phrases I'd memorized years ago.

Afterward, I think back to the me I was five years ago: the quiet American girl who had newly embraced Islam, who still lived in her parents' home, who had no idea what lay ahead. One of the early attractions of Islam—in addition to the desire to experience

Islamic culture from the inside—was that by setting up my prayer rug, *qibla* finder, Qur'ans, and other accoutrements of Islam in my room, I could put myself on the other side of the world without leaving the house. The daily rhythm of prayers, the Arabic phrases and ritual movements that went with them, even facing Mecca—all of this connected me with the daily lives of millions of people on the other side of the world. The Arabic words I labored to read in the Qur'an, admittedly mostly in transliteration since my Arabic reading skills were so limited, were simultaneously being repeated by millions of Arabs, Iranians, Turks, Pakistanis . . . the list went on. By being Muslim, I could step outside the banal familiarity of life in America and become part of a very different world. Pakistani peasants and Arab sheiks were no longer foreign creatures. I had something important in common with them: according to Islam, they were all my "brothers" and "sisters," and as such we were enjoined to help each other no matter how far apart we lived. This is why Muslims feel such solidarity with, say, the Palestinian cause even if they're not Arab, can't understand Arabic, and live thousands of miles away. These are their *brothers and sisters* under attack. The notion of being part of a world *ummah* (nation) composed of all Muslims of all different races, cultures, and languages greatly appealed to me.

Much, much later, I would form the nagging suspicion that my taste for the exotic simply reflected a compulsion to root myself *anywhere but here*. I wonder how much of that feeling had to do with not just wanting to be *somewhere* else but also to be *someone* else. Converting to Islam allows you to reinvent yourself and even take a new name if you desire. I had chosen a Muslim name, Layla Nasreddin, although I admit I almost never used it, not even among other Muslims, all of whom knew me as Lisa. It was a name I could hide behind when I didn't want to reveal my identity. "Layla" means "night" and referred, in my mind, both to the romantic tale of the ill-fated lovers Layla and Majnun (which means "crazy" or "possessed") and, being the music lover I am, Eric Clapton's famous song "Layla." I took "Nasreddin" because it means "victory of faith," and something about the assertive, even aggressive attitude it encapsulated appealed to me. Also, it is the name of Mullah Nasreddin, a famous comic character in Middle Eastern folklore.

Yes, I could take a new name of my choice, but otherwise Islam seems to have rules for everything. It seems bizarre in retrospect that I chose to embrace a religion with so many regulations governing every aspect of behavior. I always detested arbitrary rules. My school career was marred by my bitter resentment of seemingly pointless rules. I had felt the same toward my parents' attempts to lay down rules at home. I suppose I've always had issues with authority figures, although I was never openly rebellious.

Given that, why on earth would I tolerate the nitpicking rules of Islam? Why did I become obsessive-compulsive about the finer points of ritual cleanliness, worrying about whether I'd done my ablutions right? Why did I concede to faceless imams and sheikhs, many long dead, the authority to dictate to me what was and was not permissible? I suppose part of the answer is that during my childhood I never felt that religion was forced on me, while the petty rules of school and home were.

Whatever the reasons, I submitted myself utterly to the commandments of Islam. There are no laws more arbitrary and capricious than those of Allah, the cosmic dictator. Why should He care if men wear gold or silk, both forbidden in Islam? Why would He be so concerned that a believer not face Mecca while answering the call of nature? Why, indeed? In fact, not just Muslim but also Orthodox Jewish thinkers have answered this question in the same way: it is precisely *because* the rules are so arbitrary that devout believers feel compelled to obey them. *Of course* the deity's purported commands seeming to be completely arcane and pointless! This means that when you make the effort to obey them, you are truly showing Allah your love and your willingness to obey. Think of it as unfakeable evidence of one's submission.

Still, the *hijab* was difficult for me. Being very timid, I was frightened at the prospect of being so instantly identifiable as a Muslim (if less identifiable as myself). But I'd been told that I didn't have to take up all the sartorial rules all at once. I could dress "modestly" at first—which meant long, baggy clothes at all times, even in the boiling hell of the desert summers where I lived—and then move on from there once I felt that I was ready. In addition, there has been an ongoing debate between conservative and more liberal Muslims over whether covering the hair is really mandated. It's definitely required for women while praying, but at other times many Muslim women, even some who are quite pious, just don't bother. Some argue that Islam enjoins modesty and not drawing attention to oneself, and since the *hijab* draws so much attention in the West, wearing it here may actually be counterproductive. I was sympathetic to this line of thought, but I figured I would wait and see how I felt about it later on. Still I experimented, going so far as to acquire my own full-length Saudi *abaya* and some *niqab*s and even a full-size authentic Saudi *burqa*, which conceals everything but the eyes and has a flap so that you can cover them, too, if you want. I liked the idea of hiding myself completely. I even worked up the courage to wear this getup a few times in public at the huge communal Eid prayers, just to see what it was like. I knew

I wouldn't look too out of place there, since I'd seen fully covered women at such gatherings before. Admittedly, I only put the veil over my face right before I joined the crowd, since I was too self-conscious to walk around in public with my face covered. Being concealed was an interesting sensation to experience for a little while, but as soon as the time came to leave, I took off the veil, happy to be able to breathe normally again instead of through a piece of cloth. Eating, as I also found out, is also extremely difficult when wearing a *burqa*. I don't know how completely veiled Saudi women do it, since they will not even remove their coverings in a restaurant to eat.

I think it's important to describe how my conversion affected my family relationships. When I started to think about converting, I slowly isolated myself from my family—in fact, everyone I knew. I figured they wouldn't understand—this was right after September 11, 2001, remember—and I really was in no mood for arguments. I'd already studied all the ugly aspects of Islam, the things I expected they would throw in my face. Contemplating the prospect of being challenged just made me more steadfast in my intention to convert. After I actually converted, I assumed that sooner or later I'd at least tell my family but was not eager to do so. I knew they would take it badly. I wanted to spare them anger and disappointment; I wanted to spare myself bitter confrontation; I actually feared I might be disowned. No, announcing my new identity around the family hearth could wait. When I discussed this with other Muslims, they agreed with me and said that I should only reveal my new faith when I felt ready.

That day never came, and consequently I cut myself off emotionally from my family members. We still spoke regularly and sometimes did things together, but the fact that they knew nothing about what I now considered the most important thing in my life had a profoundly alienating effect on my relationship with them. This was perhaps the worst thing that could have happened, since it meant I now had nobody at all to talk to about my deepest feelings, about what was really going on in my life. Surely I had no one to talk to about my deepening, twisted sexual relationship with the imam who had converted me.

Our pattern of almost daily petting to orgasm (his, at least) at a remote house owned by the mosque in the desert could not continue indefinitely. I don't remember exactly how long it was after we'd started, perhaps a month or two, but one afternoon as we were fooling around, he asked me to recite some words in Arabic after him, which I did.

Then he told me that I was now his wife.

There is something in Islam called *misyar*, or traveler's, marriage, in which sexual activity between the parties is legitimized, but the woman gives up her right to support from the man and does not live with him. It is a new form of marriage that has become popular in the Sunni world over the past ten years, probably taking its cue from the Shi'ite *mu'tah*, or temporary marriage, in which a couple is married for a specified length of time, anywhere between a few minutes to ninety-nine years. Both *misyar* and *mu'tah* marriage are popular—not just among poor young people who lack the money to set up house in the traditional way but also among married men who want to have one or more additional wives without having to let Wife #1 know about it. This, of course, was the reason for the imam's "marriage" to me. Now he no longer had to feel guilty about what he was doing with me; it was "legal" in the eyes of Islam. Unbelievably (from my perspective today), I accepted all of this. Compounding the absurdity, he gave me, as the *mahr* (the gift a man gives a woman when they marry) the regal sum of $35 so I could purchase a bus pass. (Earlier, I'd told him I really needed one for the month and had no money.)

We became lovers fully then, and what followed I'd just as soon forget. Though he knew well that I'd never been intimate with anyone else, he didn't consider me a "true" virgin because I wasn't completely "intact," which is to say that I hadn't bled during intercourse. I'd certainly heard about such an attitude but had never experienced it up close, and it frightened me. I recalled tales about the disgrace and shame heaped upon Middle Eastern girls who failed to bleed on their wedding nights even if they were in fact virgins—hence the popularity of hymen reconstruction surgery in that part of the world.

Although we were engaging in sexual intercourse, our habits remained about the same. Almost every afternoon, the imam and I would go back to that shabby little house out in the desert. He would pick me up in his car at some obscure location far from the mosque so nobody would see us, then have me ride lying down on the back seat. At first, all we had was a towel on the floor of one of the bedrooms, but the imam soon managed to acquire a "bed" for the house, really just a mattress on a cot. This he set up so that it directly faced the mirrored doors of the closet that covered half of one wall because he enjoyed watching himself possess me. The only exceptions to this pattern were when I was menstruating, at which time Islam forbids intercourse, so we would either restrict ourselves to heavy petting or not go to the house at all.

How could a cleric justify this behavior? He explained to me that Islam, in its infinite wisdom, allowed a man up to four wives because so often, a man's desire exceeded what one woman could satisfy. Therefore Allah permitted polygyny, which was far superior to what he said Western men did, which was to have mistresses. The fact that I possessed exactly the same status as a mistress, save for the fig leaf of a *misyar* marriage that could not be substantiated because nothing had been committed to writing, never seemed to enter his mind.

A few times when his family was away, the imam actually took me to his own house, and we had sex in his bed—where he and his wife slept, I couldn't help thinking uneasily. She was a jealous woman, he had told me countless times before, so it was imperative that she never find out. I must never tell anyone. I acquiesced, of course. I was so lonely and desperate I didn't want to lose him. I think I even convinced myself that I loved him.

I didn't recognize it at the time, but he was treating me as something indistinguishable from garbage. Perhaps that was just how he was used to treating women given his conservative Jordanian background. To be sure, not all Muslim men treat women like that: some men are better than their religion. Of course, it never occurred to me that I had a right to be treated with respect and courtesy. The imam rarely complimented me and never took much interest in what would please me; he focused only on what I could do to please him. When we talked, which wasn't often anymore, he would remind me that the nature of our "marriage" was just a matter of his giving me a "good time," nothing deeper—and that I should be grateful to have that much. He always insisted that he "wanted to take care of me" and was concerned for my welfare and about looking after me in an Islamically acceptable way (though he would have phrased the last two more clumsily since his English wasn't that good). He would tell me that I should be grateful that I had "half a husband" as opposed to a "full" one because he knew many women who had none at all. The word *love* was never spoken, nor did I derive real pleasure from our sleazy assignations. When we were finished, he would drop me off somewhere near the mosque with a brusque goodbye. I should have known that I wouldn't be the only one. There was a girl in a nearby city whom he knew in every sense of that word, and there was at least one other somewhere else, but I never knew for sure how many such relationships he had. One time, he took me to see one of those other girls. I ended up, at his insistence, involved in a *ménage à trois*, and it was very uncomfortable for me. I was never jealous, though; I just felt glad that I had part of him and that he sometimes paid attention to me.

I hesitate to disclose these details, but they really capture the imam's whole attitude toward me. Although I was on the pill (which he said he "didn't trust"), he preferred to try to avoid conception by engaging in anal sex. This particular act, I knew, was *haraam* (forbidden) under Islamic law, even for heterosexual married couples, and he knew this as well as I did. I put up a couple of feeble protests, and he admitted that it wasn't allowed, but that didn't stop him. It was awful and very painful. He didn't seem to notice at all how much it hurt me, and he had absolutely no notion about how to make it hurt less. He acted the same way he did the rest of the time—he just went right to it without any preparation whatever, and I pretended to enjoy it. I still shudder at the thought. He told me on numerous occasions that he enjoyed being penetrated anally, and I wondered what this sprang from. Apparently it is not uncommon for men in conservative Muslim countries to engage in homosexual relations before marriage since social contact with the opposite sex is so thoroughly discouraged.

This story captures another grim aspect of our relationship.

When I was with the imam, I lacked all ability to stand up for myself, to say no. I submitted to almost anything he asked, no matter how degrading or painful, and even acted like I was having a good time. It was absolutely insane.

About a year or so after we first met, the imam left his job at the mosque and moved to another city about an hour and a half away. I was devastated. I suppose I shouldn't have been since he was using me so shabbily, but at the time all I could think about was how lonely I would be without him. This was ridiculous, of course—I was lonely *with* him—but I was hardly thinking clearly. He constantly warned me that if anyone found out about us, he would cut me off forever and deny he knew me, and that was enough to guarantee my silence. Through all the years of our sordid encounters, I told no one.

We continued to meet from time to time after his move. In the early days, he would travel to my city and stay at a motel. Later on, when I finally got a job and a car, I would travel to see him whenever and wherever he asked and pay for a motel room myself. It was really quite awful. He would usually ask me, once he got in the room, if I had been with anybody else. He knew I hadn't, but he had to hear me say it. After that, there would be a couple of hours of mechanical, joyless, often painful sex. Invariably he would turn on the television and proceed to pay more attention to whatever was on than to me, even while we were supposedly in the throes of passion, and I would impatiently wait for him to finish sodomizing me—that was one taste he never gave up. After two or three hours of this, sometimes less, he would shower, get dressed, pray (usually the afternoon or evening prayer), and ask me if I needed anything. I would say no, and he would either leave or direct me to leave before him so we wouldn't be seen together.

He also liked phone and online sex. He had many opportunities to indulge this taste since he was frequently on the road as a professional fund raiser. I really didn't care for it, especially when he asked me to strip for him, but as always I acquiesced. In time, he acquired yet another secret "wife," not the one he and I had visited together, and even spoke with her on the telephone while we were having video calls. By that point, I was far past caring—I just wanted the conversation and what followed to be over quickly.

Our "relationship" dragged on for years, devastating me emotionally. I hated the sneaking around, the lies. I felt terrible and worthless: I was violating everything in my ethical and moral codes, every teaching of my newfound faith—and for what? Our encounters were nothing more than meaningless physical workouts to assuage his lust, void of emotional depth and warmth. Sure, what we were doing was "legal" according to Islam, but my whole being objected to it. As time passed, we saw each other less frequently. As disgusted with the arrangement as I was, I still couldn't bring myself to end it. I constantly questioned myself: Why did I put up with this? Why was I so shy? Why couldn't I just break it off? To this day I can't believe I put up with it all. The only good thing, I suppose, was that I didn't have to live with him!

How did all of this affect my religion, the thing that had led me to the imam in the first place? Through it all, I went on following Islam as obsessively as my circumstances allowed. I attended Friday prayer regularly and tried to keep up with the five daily prayers. I worried about my large student loan, and more specifically the interest (*riba*) it carried, which Islam forbids. Someone told me that since I'd taken that on before being a Muslim it wasn't blameworthy, but I was never wholly convinced. Still, lacking the money to pay it off,

I could only hope Allah would see that I was trying the best I could. There were a couple other problems. For one thing, I owned a dog, which I had no inclination to give up. Under Islamic law, dogs are unclean; if you are licked by one, you are supposed to wash the area seven times, once with dirt. This was impossible for me, given my circumstances and my dog's keen friendliness. Fortunately, I discovered an alternative school of Islamic jurisprudence that said it was enough to wash the affected area with water. Another issue was music, which many Muslim scholars consider *haraam*. This was one opinion I knew I could not honor: I loved music and had thousands of songs in my collection. Asking me to give up one of the few things in my life that gave me any kind of joy was just too much. No, I thought (however blasphemously), I'm not really sure that Allah exists; I certainly don't know for sure that he forbids music; but I *do* know that I love music and it makes me happy. Allah will understand—or so I hoped!

Speaking of Allah, what did I really believe? I think I had convinced myself on some level that I believed, or at least was willing to give Allah the benefit of the doubt and live as if He existed—even if my doubts never stilled and I struggled with them constantly. I managed to turn them off while I was at prayer; at those times I strove to give myself over to the experience of worshiping Allah. I peppered my speech with stock Islamic phrases like "*in sha 'Allah*" ("if Allah wills") and "*Alhamdulillah*" ("praise be to Allah"). If I couldn't say them around my family, I said them in my mind. I trained myself to believe that all things were the will of Allah and that he would take care of me, and that's when I came closest to real belief. When I was really desperate or depressed or fearful, I would mutter a prayer for Allah's help. It was never more complex than a couple of words, yet right afterward I might feel a warm presence or at least a lifting of my mood. I suppose that when I prayed, I let go of the conflicted feelings that were overwhelming me, if only for a moment, which in turn engendered the peaceful feeling. Even so, the trick worked only when I was especially upset or frightened.

My ongoing relationship with the imam eroded my initial enthusiasm for Islam after the first year or so; between that and the waning of interest often seen among new converts, I began to slack off in my observance. At first I felt terrible when I couldn't do all my prayers on time; eventually I felt all right if I managed to do at least one almost every day. (I later learned that enormous numbers of supposedly observant Muslims have trouble managing to perform all their prayers—it's probably the most difficult of the five pillars of Islam to observe fully.)

But I always fasted during Ramadan, continued reading the Qur'an on a regular basis, and kept up my Islamic studies. Still, I could not help wishing that there was a Reform Islam, along the lines of Reform Judaism, where you could shuck off all those onerous rules while still affirming the core tenets of the faith. My reading habits during this period were no less incongruous; I devoured secular books that cast doubt on traditional Islamic history and the authenticity of the Qur'an without weakening— consciously, at least—my belief in Islamic tenets. I had developed a knack for compartmentalization back in my early days when I would read something like Ibn Warraq's *Why I Am Not a Muslim*, take a break to pray, and then return to the book. I could read books spelling out all the textual problems with the Qur'an and the historical worthlessness of the *hadith* collections and the traditional account of Muhammad's life, *agree with them*, and then hit a switch in my brain and go back to being a more or less faithful Muslim. Needless to say, this was completely untenable, and on some level I knew it, but I couldn't admit it to myself. I suppose I wasn't emotionally ready to leave Islam.

In 2006, I even went through a period of religious revival. I attended an Eid prayer that year and vowed that I would try much harder to fulfill my religious obligations. I would pray five times a day, even if circumstances were not perfect or I wasn't absolutely sure I was following all the rules. If I still couldn't bring myself to wear my *hijab* to work, I would find a way to pray there sometimes. I would study the Qur'an in Arabic and go to the mosque more often. I joined a small group of female American converts that had just formed at the mosque, and we would meet together and discuss our difficulties being Muslim in American society, as well as study more about Islam. It would be all right, I thought. I'd find a way to harmonize Islam with my life and beliefs.

Looking back, I suspect this whole effort was an attempt to still my uneasiness and my growing doubts. They'd always been there, as I've mentioned, but they felt sharper now. It seemed my mind was being torn apart by trying to hold onto belief while simultaneously accepting the legitimacy of the feminist, historical, and other critiques of Islam I'd been reading. I couldn't make it all fit together. I knew all about the rampant sexism in traditional understandings of Islam and deplored its misogyny, but at the same time I had to admit that it was inherent in the sources, the Qur'an and *hadith*. I felt similarly conflicted with hellfire-and-brimstone attitudes toward nonbelievers and heretics, as I did with traditional Islam's stance on any number of subjects ranging from slavery to *jihad* to the position of Islam in Muslim countries. Yes, moderates could try to explain them away, but fundamentalists could easily demonstrate that the positions I found abhorrent were fully supported by the texts.

I'm not sure when I first seriously considered leaving Islam. I'd always had doubts and difficulties, but I dreamed I would finally stumble one day onto the perfect synthesis of Islam and my own liberal ethical and moral inclinations. But as time went by and I learned yet more about the texts and the way Islam had been interpreted by almost every scholar, imam, sheikh, mufti, mullah, and ayatollah, my hopes for finding a "liberal Islam" dimmed. What right had I, a female Western convert of no great learning, to contradict 1,400 years of tradition and challenge the most knowledgeable Muslim scholars?

As my hopes for salvaging anything out of Islam began to wither, I had to confront the fact that my faith had *always* been built on sand. Had I ever really believed, or had I been fooling myself? The longer I agonized, the more I suspected the latter was the case. Yet I could never fully admit that to myself. I clung to what was left of my faith, a last-gasp effort to keep something I'd been a part of for six long years.

Once real cracks appeared in my resolve, they didn't take long to spread. I found myself beginning to frequent freethinker, ex-Muslim, and atheist Web sites, even while I was struggling desperately to hold on to my tattered faith. I realized that some part of me *liked* the infidels' attitudes; when it came to Islam, they said the things I longed to say. They denounced outrages like Islamic misogyny wholeheartedly without having to qualify their statements with remarks like, "but that is only because Islam has been misinterpreted or misused." No, they denounced the whole rotten thing, root and branch, and I found that refreshing. Imagine being able to denounce the Qur'an for the atrocious verses it contained without having to pretzel one's brain trying to reconcile the "perfect" Word of Allah with modern notions of human rights.

Imagine being able to condemn certain of Muhammad's actions unreservedly (assuming they actually happened as claimed, mind), without simultaneously trying to defend the Prophet's honor and "perfect" example through some treacly appeal to relativism. How bracing it would be to leave all that nonsense behind.

Finally, I just snapped. With a lot of help from people online, I realized that I couldn't keep up the masquerade. I admitted to myself that I really didn't believe—that in all likelihood, I never truly had. Maybe I'd been fooling myself for the past six years. The hurdle that remained was the most difficult: giving up Islam for good.

One of my last acts as a Muslim was *salat al-istikhara*, the prayer asking Allah to show his guidance on a matter. Paradoxical as it may sound, *I asked Allah whether I should give up my faith*. It probably helped that after I said the prayer I went to sleep; often, people think more clearly after a good rest.

I guess Allah decided that I should give up Islam because that's what I did. The Qur'an says that only those whom Allah wills believe. Apparently, that group does not include me! I was one of those whom Muhammad said would leave the religion as an arrow goes through game.

Levity aside, the last year or so has been quite difficult. I've had to wrestle with a cascade of feelings, even as I face the fact that I spent so many years driving myself crazy over something so utterly ridiculous.

I've started reading the Qur'an again, curious how it would seem now that I no longer believe. I find myself flabbergasted at how pedestrian and banal it truly is. I've been through the text so many times that its words hold no surprises; what strikes me now is how little is really new or impressive. Set aside the dire depictions of hellfire and the pretty pictures of paradise, pass by the constant invocations of the Last Day when humankind will stand before Allah and be judged, and there is really not much left. Some retold stories from the Bible, some stereotyped retellings of the legends of the prophets, some legal matters, some aphorisms and proverbs that seem profound yet encode no more than common sense, some exhortations to give thanks to Allah and perform prayers and give charity and fight in the way of Allah—it is all thuddingly repetitive, surely nothing that a seventh-century Arab speaker could not have come up with on his own without divine assistance. So much for the notion that the Qur'an is so perfect that it simply *must* be the very word of Allah!

It's astonishing what exorbitant and extravagant claims are made for this book by Muslims. Even in the original Arabic, which contains some nice poetry, there is nothing in the text to warrant it.

The more time passes, the more perplexed I become about why exactly I chose to convert to Islam. That's one of the reasons I wrote this lengthy account: I'm trying to sort it all out in my own mind. It's been a very draining process. Perhaps I have learned a few things about myself. One thing is sure—after reviewing the unhappy history of my past several years, there is absolutely no chance whatever that I will ever return to Islam. There is no way I will put myself through that torture again.

No, I've decided that I'm happy as I am, without religion. I can only hope that my experience will prove interesting or useful to somebody. I believe far fewer things than I once did, but I truly believe that no experience is wasted if I, or you, or someone else can learn from it.

Lisa Bauer now attends graduate school. In the third and final part of the story of her encounter with Islam, which will be published in the next issue of Free Inquiry, *she explores Islam's effects.*

SUBJECTION AND ESCAPE
PART 3
AN AMERICAN WOMAN'S
MUSLIM JOURNEY
Lisa Bauer

In the third and final part of this series, Lisa Bauer explains how the combination of her devotion to Islam and certain characteristics of her personality almost destroyed her.—EDS.

Countless commentators have offered general reasons for objecting to Islam—it's misogynistic, medieval, theocratic, and so on. I agree, and one can read innumerable critiques along these lines by Muslim, ex-Muslim, and non-Muslim writers. I wish to take a more personal approach. What was it about Islam as a religion that combined with my psychology to create the sad, terrified, timid young woman I was—and, truth be told, to some extent still am?

It's not just that Islam is horrific in itself. Mix its teachings, rules, and general ethos with my own sensitive personality—add in my pathetic tale of being sexually exploited by the religious authority figure I trusted to guide me in Islam's path—and you may come to understand how the experience made me such an emotional wreck. Someone better adjusted than I was might have been able to leave Islam with only mild regrets, pausing just long enough to curse the faith before moving on. Vulnerable as I was to begin with, Islam proved a soul-destroying experience—if the atheist I now am may

145

use *soul* to denote my personality, deepest thoughts, and emotions. Indeed, I am far from certain Islam is finished with me. I do not know when its emotional effects will end.

If my Muslim journey did not destroy me, it came close.

Looking back, I suspect that one of Islam's greatest attractions lay in how well it complemented my personality at the time. I was very shy. Islam values modesty, especially in women. I thought I was worthless. Islam teaches that humans are nothing before the majesty and power of Allah. I feared other people and new experiences. Islam counsels women to stay safe and protected inside the home. For these reasons, Islam was almost certainly the worst religion I could have chosen—it reinforced the weakest aspects of my personality. Indeed it *sacralized* them, telling me that my flaws were just what the Almighty Creator of the Universe most cherished in me. Instead of encouraging me to attack my weaknesses, it bid me to be proud of them.

I wish to examine each of these traits in detail, the better to understand how Islam, or Islam as I then understood it, preyed upon them. Of course, "Islam" is not a conscious being. It might be thought of as a mind virus, to borrow a phrase from Richard Dawkins: pernicious, perhaps, but not purposeful. Still, what rendered me so susceptible?

First, Islam values self-abnegation in the face of Allah. Believers prostrate themselves each day before the Almighty in a posture of absolute servility. Not for nothing does Islam refer to believers as "slaves of Allah." Islam rejects the Christian image of believers as children of God; Allah is not a parent but a master, with absolute power over his slaves who are nothing before his infinite might and majesty. Allah is an absolute dictator, far more so than in Christianity. His will cannot be questioned; one can only submit to it. A good Muslim expresses no desire or plan for the future without adding *"In sha' Allah"* ("If Allah wills"). Not infrequently this gives rise to a passive, fatalistic mind-set, often with pernicious consequences. Allah has already mapped out each person's fate. We are like grains of sand blown by the wind and of no greater importance in the eyes of Allah.

This self-abnegating woman found that oddly comforting. I already thought of myself as inconsequential. I don't know the roots of my miserable self-esteem and lack of self-confidence—I can't recall ever feeling otherwise. Perhaps it sprang in part from my inability to make friends. If I couldn't make friends, it must be my fault. I must be the sort of person nobody would want to be around. Add to that my feelings of helplessness whenever I confronted a new or frightening situation. If all things were Allah's will, then I needn't worry so much about what I could and couldn't do. If I was meant to do something, Allah would make it happen regardless of my shortcomings.

I seized upon Islamic ideas of female modesty. When the Qur'an teaches women to cover themselves and not "display their adornment," this is no mere counsel against vanity and self-assertion. Women are taught not to make themselves too attractive for fear of arousing uncontrollable male desire. This was fine by me, since I regarded myself as completely unattractive already. Islamic rules on female dress meant I could hide what I thought of as my disgusting body in loose, long clothes, even if I didn't quite have the courage to cover my hair.

Modesty refers to one's attitude as well as one's outward appearance. Again that appealed to my faults—I was so intensely shy that I was an anomaly even among the other women at the mosque. I recall at least one telling me that my extreme modesty was something favored by Allah. I presume that a born *Muslimah* as timid as I would simply remain at home rather than socialize at the mosque. After all, women, unlike men, are not required to attend prayers at the mosque, and one tradition even states that the best prayer for women is that offered within the most private part of her home. (Ironically, many of the women I met at the mosque were rather outgoing by community standards or else I would not have met them there.) The idea of becoming invisible appealed to me. Occasionally, I fantasized about living in Saudi Arabia or some Gulf country where I could go about fully veiled, my personhood obliterated.

Still, as much as I yearned to hide myself, I also longed for some sort of recognition, an acknowledgment that I existed and had made an impression on somebody. It was a prescription for hapless openness.

I think one of the reasons I converted was the hope that I would finally find true friends. Somewhere in my mind also lurked the idea that by joining Islam, I might somehow find a husband. My high school and university experience had convinced me I would never find one by myself. Perhaps an arranged marriage would solve the problem, sidestepping the whole business of meeting people and dating. I genuinely thought that might be the only way I would ever find a man. Islamic communities are one of the few settings in the West where such things occur with any frequency. In addition, Islam teaches that husbands must support their wives financially in exchange for obedience, and this comforted me. So tattered was my self-confidence that despite my intelligence and my university degree, I feared I might not be able to support myself.

Even while my feminist side recoiled from the prospect of owing obedience to a husband, I clung to the thought that if my parents cut me off or disowned me because of my conversion to Islam, I could submit to an arranged marriage and be provided for. Of course, that ignored the very real question of what I would do if my husband later decided to divorce me, which Islam gave him the unilateral power to do. I wasn't thinking that far ahead!

Muslim women are often taught to fear and hide from strange men, especially in more conservative Islamic societies. Here my discussion returns to the Jordanian Arab imam who first converted me and then took me for his *misyar* "wife." Directly and indirectly, he very much encouraged in me the attitude that I should be timid and reclusive, avoiding most contact with the outside world. Interactions with other Muslim women were all right, but meeting and speaking to strange men should be avoided at all costs. Self-serving on his part as this was, it fit with my antisocial leanings, and I was more than happy to comply. He knew that I felt I must hide my newfound faith from my parents, whom I imagined would be quite hostile. Yet in his mind, it was much better that I continued to live under their roof. He encouraged me not to go out too much, except for necessities. Given that I hardly ever went out anyway, except to the mosque and university (I was taking several college classes at the time), this seemed a small imposition.

As it happens, my sexual attitudes had always been fairly conservative, so I found no difficulty in embracing Islam's rigorous "no sexual contact outside of marriage" rules. This went by the wayside once the imam started to take an interest in me (religious hypocrisy when it comes to sex—what else is new?). Ironic as this may seem now, Islam's rigid sexual mores were one of its great attractions for me. I loathed the way some men, especially those with money, authority, or fame, took advantage of women. Restricting sex within the bounds of marriage would provide a safeguard against that, I imagined. Of course, as I learned very painfully, marriage does nothing to prevent men from treating women as objects. The power differential between spouses in a traditional Islamic marriage is so great that the woman is essentially her husband's slave. Yet I still harbored, even cherished, my idealized Western notion of marriage as a partnership between two essentially equal spouses. From this sprang my reluctance to place myself "under the control of a man" in marriage. Yet I truly never conceived what that might actually mean until I experienced it for myself.

The imam was likely attracted to my timid, quiet nature. Clearly I could be trusted not to talk about what was going on between us. When we were together, I became cringingly subservient, willing to do anything to please him as I imagined a good Muslim wife should, no matter how degrading or unpleasant it might be. I would respond to his abuses by apologizing for my failure to anticipate his whims. I felt grateful that he, busy as he was with a family and the duties of the mosque, deigned to spend a couple of hours with me in the afternoons or evenings. (It is worth noting that his real wife, an Arab like him, was not nearly so subservient—she was never shy about making her desires and displeasures known!)

Sadly, I *was* genuinely grateful to have what I did of this man. Time and again I thanked Allah for guiding me to him. I had convinced myself that he was the best I could hope for, indeed better than I deserved. He wasn't physically abusive (leaving aside his enthusiasm for anal sex), and he seemed interested in me. Despite his warnings that this was all just a "good time" to him and that I shouldn't get too attached, in my loneliness and vulnerability I think I eventually convinced myself that I felt real love for him.

In the early stages of our relationship, I was painfully aware that our actions were grossly *haraam* (forbidden), and this caused me intense guilt. In my loneliness, I found myself ignoring my own moral and ethical standards—anything to be with him! But then came our *misyar* marriage, after which I felt that Islam had legitimized our relationship. I had no real objection to being somebody's second, third, or fourth wife—beggars couldn't be choosers, I figured. Even so, *misyar* marriage didn't allay all my misgivings. I still felt guilty that he was betraying his wife and children with me. I detested that we had to hide our relationship, but since what we were doing was permissible under Islamic law I somehow managed to swallow my objections and continue on. He was the Islamic scholar who had been educated at elite Islamic universities, and if he said our arrangement was okay, then who was I to argue?

I must point out that awful as he was, the imam merely personified Islamic values, at least as they are understood in certain Arab Muslim cultures. A Muslim man from a more liberal background might have had more enlightened attitudes toward women and marriage, but assuming he was devout enough, he would no doubt value modesty, obedience, and a retiring nature as qualities to cherish in a prospective spouse. That attitude toward women is so deeply ingrained that even fairly modern Muslim men from such cultures who enjoy the company of independent, outspoken Western women will still seek out these qualities when it comes to looking for a wife. Such is the culture, formed in no small part by the religion.

Because I wanted to be an obedient, submissive *Muslimah*, I found myself acquiescing to picayune Islamic regulations that I might otherwise never have dreamed of honoring. A woman shouldn't travel alone, defined as going farther than about ninety miles without a male guardian to "protect" her. (The distance was calculated from how far a camel could travel in a day, demonstrating just how ancient this rule is!) At the very least, she needs permission from a man to travel. Instead of being angry about this, I accepted it, actually phoning the imam on a couple of occasions for permission to travel to a nearby city with my family! In addition, a married woman should not leave her home without her husband's permission. This standard could not be realized fully—we didn't live together, after all—but he told me to stay home as much as possible, which I did. Other rules restrict prayer, fasting, sex, and even touching the Qur'an during menstruation, and I accepted those too, repulsed as I was by them. A Muslim submits to Allah in all things, and since I wanted to do my best to live up to the new religion I believed I'd freely chosen, I obeyed even the most archaic and misogynistic rules.

Muslims are taught to patiently accept whatever disappointments and disasters life may bring. This too I found weirdly congenial, though the fatalism and passivity Islam encouraged was the last thing someone as fearful as I might need. When I was a child, I'd had bold dreams for my future. As I got older, I lost my grip on those dreams. It wasn't that the ambitions of my childhood were replaced by more realistic and attainable goals. Rather, I became so convinced that I was incapable that they disappeared entirely. I believed muddling through life was the best I could hope for, an attitude Islam cruelly exploited. Islam also teaches that a woman's highest honor is to be a wife and mother, so I began to think that that, too, was the most I could aspire to. I lost hope that I would ever amount to anything . . . and yet I felt guilty about that. Teachers and parents had told me for years that I had great potential, and here I was throwing it all away. When I become emotional about the years

I wasted as a Muslim, I wonder how much I'm also mourning the loss of my dreams.

Living without hope is very hard.

Islam teaches that humans should be eternally grateful to Allah for everything, since he is the creator and sustainer of the universe. The proper attitude of a believer is to be *shakir* (grateful), as contrasted with its antonym, *kafir*, which means "ungrateful" as well as "unbeliever." No matter what difficulties and hardships a Muslim faces, she must always remember to be grateful to Allah; what happens in this world is nothing compared with the eternal rewards and punishments in the hereafter. The effects of this can be disturbing. Believers will thank Allah profusely for the tiniest crumbs of luck thrown their way even as the rest of their world falls apart. Still I could understand its appeal. During low moments, I would remind myself to thank Allah that I was alive, that my parents and family were well, that I'd found Islam, and so on, small things that I tended to overlook. Even a drink of water or a piece of cake was something to treasure and for which to give thanks.

Sometimes, while I inventoried what I was fortunate enough to have and thanked Allah for it all, I wondered about those who were not so lucky. What of devout Muslims who died or were gravely injured in some horrific natural disaster? What of those who lived in grinding poverty? Was Allah looking out for me and not them? Yet everything that happened was the inscrutable will of Allah, and no one had the right to question what he might choose to grant each of his slaves. Imagine a cruel and unpredictable dictator giving you an expensive gift while ordering the person next to you to be executed. Standing before him, you probably are not going to spend much time pondering how unfair and arbitrary the situation is; you're going to be glad that you were not the one executed! In short order, you will be on your knees in a posture of servile gratitude, cringingly acknowledging his kind magnanimity. When the Qur'an instructs the believers to always "fear" Allah, it is speaking quite literally.

Still, why was it so unfair? There must have been millions of Muslims more worthy of my (relative) wealth and (relative) good fortune than I; why were they being "tested" so frightfully? They might receive their reward in paradise, but that promise rang a bit hollow. I suppose that introspective as I was, I spent too much time musing about things like that, but the sheer injustice of it all always distressed me.

As my faith wavered, I began exploring atheist Web sites in earnest. One of the sites I found especially intriguing was RichardDawkins. net. Despite feeling a bit irritated by what I felt was the strident tone of some of the items I read there, the site's frequent updates meant that some new article about religion was always being posted and discussed at length. Many of the commenters impressed me with their evident intelligence and thoughtfulness. Strangely enough, I had not previously heard of Richard Dawkins. In all my reading, I'd never even opened the book that was the basis for the site *The God Delusion*, aside from one brief glance in a bookstore. I recall being unimpressed by what I gathered was an argument that "science shows God is unlikely to exist." Fortunately, I resolved to keep an open mind.

What happened next would change my life. Again. But I get ahead of myself.

As I look back from my hard-won vantage of unbelief, I see so many red flags I should have spotted then. Wasn't it *too easy* to convert to Islam? When I first entered the mosque seven years ago, neither the imam nor anybody else seriously questioned my knowledge of Islam, how confident I was in my decision, or whether I actually understood what I was getting into. All that was really required was that I stand up and recite the *shahadah*, the testimony of faith, before at least two witnesses. By contrast, many other religions require potential converts to undergo some course of study sometimes lasting a year or more. Admittedly, I was so determined to convert at that point that even the prospect of undergoing a lengthy "apprenticeship" might not have dissuaded me, but I have to wonder how attractive Islam would have remained after seeing it from the inside for several months. There is also the issue of people converting who know *nothing* about Islam, a factor that may help explain the fairly high percentage of converts who end up abandoning the faith. You can convert on the spur of the moment— in the heat of passion, as it were—and only realize much later that you've let yourself in for something you did not anticipate. (This is starting to sound like an ill-considered Las Vegas wedding!) At the time of my own conversion, I did not understand fully what I was embracing; but the fact that I managed to overcome my deep fears and find the courage to go to the mosque, a terribly forbidding place to me at the time, suggests that I was completely serious. I'd given a great deal of thought to the notion of converting to this strange, complex religion, and as a result I felt obligated to honor my vow by dutifully following the rules and adopting the mental attitudes of Islam.

Among those attitudes is a near obsession with death and the afterlife. Serious Christians believe in a world to come, but Islam goes an extra step. The Qur'an and other Islamic texts teach that this life is nothing but play and amusement, a brief prelude to the terrors of the Last Day and eternal reward or punishment in the hereafter. A good Muslim should keep death in mind at all times, the better to keep to the straight path. This dovetailed perversely with my own longtime tendency to obsess about death; I'd been melancholy and depressive even as a small child. Back then, growing up in no particular religion (an attempt at Catholic indoctrination took place later on), I'd worry anxiously about what would happen after death. If anything, my lack of belief in an afterlife *contributed* to my preoccupation with what lay beyond the grave. Later on, no matter how sincerely I convinced myself that I had embraced Islam, the part about the hereafter never quite stuck for me. The Qur'an endlessly repeated that I could be certain of a life after death, and as a believing Muslim I was supposed to draw deep comfort from that. But here my carefully cultivated attempt at faith failed me—I could never really, fully believe it. I could "believe" that Allah would look after me and make everything all right *today*, if that was his will. But when it came to belief in an afterlife, well . . . I didn't know how the imam or people at the mosque could be so sure that there would in fact be *anything* on the other side. That issue being unresolved in my mind, my new religion's incessant focus on death and the afterlife merely heightened my distress.

One aspect of Islam that renders it so incomprehensible to many Westerners of Christian background is its cornucopia of incredibly detailed rules for *everything*—from which foot to use when entering the mosque to the proper way to slaughter an animal. One must not defecate in the direction of Mecca; men must not wear silk or gold; one must not drink or eat off of gold utensils; and so on. Specifically religious rituals such as prayer and ablutions are painstakingly elaborated in voluminous works written and added to by dozens of scholars. This conception of an all-encompassing and insanely detailed sacred law is familiar from Judaism, if not all that widely followed today, but it is almost absent from Christianity. Why does it matter whether you wash your face or your arms first when doing *wudu'* (ablution)? The traditional justification is that Islam is not just a *religion* in the way that term is often used in the West but a way of life. Far from something you can put away in a little box and take out once a week at the mosque, it is something to be lived, touching every aspect of life.

In theory, this could be a good thing—every action could remind one of Allah, especially with all the specialized *du'a*s (supplications) that faithful Muslims often recite to go along with their actions. But for me, the actual experience of trying to live my life in accordance with the divine law of Islam was sharply unpleasant. Like many converts, I obsessed over the rules, terrified that my prayer might not be accepted because I'd had a hole in my sock, or perhaps I hadn't done my *wudu'* absolutely correctly. Born Muslims are often more casual about such things, though this sometimes leads their more punctilious neighbors to criticize them for not doing it right.

I developed an obsessive-compulsive focus on ritual correctness. Sometimes I would spend more energy worrying whether I had passed gas (which renders one ritually impure) than concentrating on my prayers. Needless to say, one can't live like that for very long. Either one learns to be less obsessive over the details, or one gives up the entire practice. I ended up doing both, though not at the same time—first I found myself slackening in my observance, much to my own disappointment. Later I decided (rationalized?) that the minutiae mattered less than what my *intention* had been—after all, Islam puts great store on the *niyah* (intention), without which any act of worship is void and worthless.

Why did I subject myself to rules I often found arbitrary, sometimes even ridiculous? That was what Islam, as I knew it, required. I had made a permanent, public commitment to this religion and I intended to follow through with it. Islam is very emphatic about the importance of loyalty—loyalty toward the religion as well as the loyalty of Muslims to one another. Since all Muslims are brothers and sisters, leaving the religion means turning your back on them. I think of myself as being a loyal person and also a stubborn one in the sense that once I make a decision about something important, I am inclined to follow through to the proverbial bitter end.

The worst of it was that Islam had convinced me that all these rules and attitudes were in fact things I had freely chosen for myself. Having chosen to embrace Islam of my own free will, I had therefore chosen to follow its regulations. I wanted to honor the promise I'd made to Allah and to myself to be the best *Muslimah* I could be, circumstances permitting.

Like any world religion, Islam employs such elements as rituals, art, and sacred stories to appeal to the emotions and thus attract and retain members. A sensitive and often emotional young woman, I proved painfully susceptible to their influence. One major factor in my conversion had been the awe-inducing impact of Islamic art and architecture—*what* had caused these people to create such beauty? Islamic rituals like the *adhan* (call to prayer) affected me tremendously as a fresh convert; hearing the *adhan* recited live in the mosque for the first time was an overwhelming experience. I was also mesmerized by the rhetorical power and sweep of the Qur'an, ridiculous as that may seem today. After repeated readings, it spoke to me on a profoundly emotional level. Recitations of it in Arabic could bring me almost to tears, never mind that I didn't understand the words. It was like music, I thought, although it is considered highly offensive to compare the noble profession of Qur'an reciting with mere singing! Being a part of the Friday *jumu'ah* (congregational) prayer was stirring also: I was part of a global multitude united in the worship of Allah. For similar reasons, I was moved by photographs or television news clips showing millions of pilgrims on the *hajj* crying out to Allah with all their might. These people had pinned all their hopes and dreams on their deity. How could I say they weren't right, ignorant as I was? Who was I to be so cruel as to declare that it was all for naught?

Finally I asked myself: of all the things Islam had come to mean for me, how much of it beyond my initial decision to accept the faith genuinely represented a *choice*? I certainly didn't feel free to jettison the aspects of Islamic law I didn't particularly care for. What right had I, an ignorant young American female convert, to question the consensus of thousands of knowledgeable scholars who had devoted their lives to the finer points of Islamic jurisprudence across the centuries? This brings up a yet larger question: to what extent are *any* believers actually free when it comes to deciding what to accept and what to reject? If the believer is absolutely convinced that the religion requires her to do or profess X, Y, and Z, she will do her best to rationalize this in her own mind, even embracing beliefs and actions that would be abhorrent under other circumstances. Sex segregation was something I generally opposed, yet I accepted women's prayer sections unthinkingly.

Granted, I wouldn't accept just *everything* that some lunatic might claim in the name of Islam—I found Islamic fundamentalism utterly repulsive. I still had my liberal principles, however submerged. Blowing yourself up to kill innocent civilians or crashing airplanes into buildings or stoning adulteresses were all wicked, evil deeds, and none of them had anything to do with the Islam I imagined myself striving to follow. Yet was that response too pat? The fanatics knew their Islamic texts and traditions, too! On what basis could I deny their legitimacy? I couldn't, really. And on what basis could I claim that my understanding of Islam, not theirs, was the correct one? Like any religion, Islam consists ultimately of what Muslims say and do, and if a substantial number of them embrace (for example) disgustingly archaic attitudes toward women—based in no small part on what the Qur'an and the traditions of the Prophet actually say—then how can an ignorant new convert contradict them? How can a newcomer reliably decide among interpretations?

For all these reasons, I found the act of finally leaving Islam terribly difficult. I felt I was betraying someone or something. Not Allah, since I no longer believed in him by the time I made the break. Perhaps I felt most that I was betraying myself and my vow to remain Muslim. I was like a wife reluctant to break her solemn vows by leaving an unhappy marriage. I imagined that sticking with my faith against all obstacles might prove that I was sincere. Giving up would mean acknowledging that I'd been wrong, that I'd wasted my time in futile prayers and fasting. I'd put so much of myself into Islam; leaving would be an acknowledgement that it was all for naught. Moreover, I felt badly about turning my back on the Muslim friends I'd made, though we weren't especially close. I would be betraying the most important thing in *their* lives, and that distressed me. I might even have felt a twinge of guilt about deserting the imam, though I had long since had my fill of his thoughtless treatment of me.

Leaving Islam may have been the hardest thing I ever did—yet I saw no other option if I sought to be intellectually honest with myself.

One other factor influenced my ultimate decision to forsake Islam for atheism. During the days when my internal struggle between faith and skepticism was near its height, I saw an announcement that Richard Dawkins would be giving a lecture not far from where I lived. I decided to go. Why not? It was free, and he might not come this way again. Perhaps I could even lend a surreal touch to the proceedings by showing up in my *hijab*, making the point that some Muslims are open-minded enough to want to hear "the opposition" for themselves! And that is just what I did—a most unusual move for me, given how timid I usually was about displaying outward signs of my Islam. I thought the incongruity was just too delicious to pass up.

By its very strangeness, the notion helped me find the courage to carry it out. I attended the lecture in full *hijab,* and none of the atheists gathered there attacked me, insulted me, or (as far as I could tell) even noticed me. That was a small revelation in itself: the experience of discovering *something* about which I had no reason to fear.

The lecture was interesting enough, although in keeping with my observant demeanor I refrained from applauding or laughing. It just would not do for a devout *Muslimah* to join in laughter at the ridicule of religious practices! As the speech continued, I sensed that Dawkins might be more understanding and less dismissive than his reputation as the world's most famous atheist suggested. By the time I left to go home, I had somehow conceived the idea of writing to him and sharing my own doubts. This was very much out of the ordinary for me; never before had I wanted to write to an author or any other well-known figure. Besides, I was a little nothing— what were the odds that a famous scientist would read what I had to say? Still, I had the feeling that he might be sympathetic to my plight, and I very much wanted to share my feelings about religion with *somebody* who might be able to understand, even a complete stranger. (Leave aside for the moment the evidence of my relationship with the imam that my intuitions regarding whom to trust were not to be relied on.)

But in the case of Dawkins, I was only writing a letter—well, an e-mail. I knew that he read at least some of his mail, for he frequently made note of letters that readers had written him. I wrote carefully, fretting about how ridiculous it would probably sound. When the e-mail was done, I asked myself, *What's the worst that can happen?* and hit "Send." *At least I've managed to write down how I feel,* I thought.

Words cannot express how shocked I was when Dawkins *responded* to my plaintive e-mail. I could hardly believe that somebody that prominent actually expressed concern and support for me! He offered to send me some books, his own and a couple by Ayaan Hirsi Ali, which I gratefully accepted.

When the books arrived, I actually broke down and wept. I simply couldn't believe that a total stranger could be so kind to me. I wrote Dawkins again, thanking him profusely.

Overwhelmed with gratitude, I quickly set about reading the books, one after another. Certainly they gave me more to think about. And though I'd read much of the literature critical of Islam before, immersing myself in it now massively increased my dissatisfaction with Islam. It helped me understand and articulate to myself, if nobody else, exactly what I personally found reprehensible and untenable about that—or any—religion.

Looking back, it's little short of incredible that the mind virus known as Islam held me in its thrall for so many years. Given my own vulnerabilities and the way that faith exploited them, it is to some degree understandable. Yes, I now feel anger, but directed at whom? Islam, after all, is just a religion, a set of beliefs and rituals and laws, a particular ethos. It doesn't have a mind or will of its own. It didn't *intend* to make me a miserable basket case—that just happened. I suppose that I am angry at myself for not seeing through the whole charade far earlier, but again, my history and personal weaknesses left me especially vulnerable to Islam's lure. Of course, the imam deserves plenty of anger for having taken advantage of a fragile, vulnerable, frightened young woman and leaving her an emotional wreck. Yet even his actions were largely informed by his faith as he understood it. Which deserves greater blame, the imam or his religion? I can't say; I suspect they're inextricable. In any case, I don't feel any hatred toward him, just anger mixed with a good deal of regret—even, perhaps, a bit of pity.

I can only hope that the combined effect of Islam, the imam, and my own personality doesn't finally end up destroying me. It came close, and in my darkest moments I fear it may yet prevail. Still, I hope that my horrific experience has offered me an opportunity to learn and to change. Now I can try to change the traits that left me so susceptible, without Islam or the imam holding me back and keeping me mired in the same old attitudes and habits. My future path will be difficult, but I hope that I will emerge a different and better person—one with increased understanding and compassion gained from bitter experience.

Lisa Bauer is now in graduate school.

WHY I AM
NOT A LUDDITE

Kristi DeMeester

It's a Tuesday afternoon, and my eleventh-grade students are booting up the computers in my school's computer lab to begin research for a recently assigned paper. They chat with one another casually as they log in and open their Internet browsers to begin work. I marvel as I watch them swiftly maneuvering through websites, online databases, and the school's word-processing program with ease. As they open and minimize multiple screens to copy and paste text into three separate documents, they don't think twice about what they are doing or how they learned to do it. Impressed as I am with their skills, I expect nothing less of them when assignments ask them to utilize technology.

Most elementary schools have been offering some sort of computer instruction since the late 1980s; however, during my own elementary school years in the early 1990s—a period of great advancement in technology—the strictly religious Pentecostal private school I attended forbade the use of computers. Year after year, students would graduate from our small school and pack their bags for university or look forward to beginning first jobs—but quickly realize that because their church had forbidden them access to computers, they lacked a skill necessary for success in academia or the workplace. Many of these students eventually dropped out of college and, feeling defeated, returned home to take low-paying part-time jobs or to marry. Others found themselves struggling to adapt to a world that demanded experience with technology; all too often, these students missed out on important opportunities because of their limited experience.

Computers—and computer programs, especially—have presented me with unique challenges in recent years when I've been asked to write research papers in Microsoft Word, create presentations in PowerPoint, or make spreadsheets in Excel. I still struggle with adapting to new technologies, and I can't help but wonder if this is because my church's private school never provided me (or my classmates) with computer instruction. Parents and teachers in Pentecostal churches and other private schools that still do not provide computer instruction must understand that as their children and students move on to universities, two-year colleges, trade schools, or careers, they will be asked to utilize technology in their work. By avoiding the so-called worldly and tempting computer, institutions like my Pentecostal church school are placing significant limitations on their students' ability to succeed in a technologically driven world.

LEARNING THE RULES

Whenever someone joined my church, he or she had to begin abiding by certain rules. As a woman, I could not cut my hair because it served as a covering for my modesty; I could not wear makeup because it belonged to the world, and I needed to maintain my purity; I could not wear jewelry because such unnecessary adornment was a product of vanity; my skirts had to pass my knees. Pants and shorts were not allowed because such garments belonged to men; my shirts could not be sleeveless lest I draw lascivious attention to my body. Granted, these rules applied to the entire female congregation, not just to me; we were all expected to follow them or else God would demonstrate his displeasure. The men had a separate set of rules concerning dress, and there were other rules the entire congregation had to follow.

Televisions were not allowed in members' homes. With its images of sinful premarital sex, violence, and fast lifestyles, television could influence the mind and tempt the faithful toward a damning lifestyle. To have a television in one's home suggested that a family engaged in loose behavior, what the church called "living in the world." If a child played at another family's house and noticed a television, that shocking fact would most certainly be revealed to the visiting child's parents, and the accused family would become the source of nasty church gossip.

Movies—regardless of content—were also off-limits. For reasons similar to those for the ban on television, movies were considered to be of the world, tempting the viewer with sexual acts, ungodly decisions, and violence.

The church deemed computers the gateway to sin because they linked the user to the Internet. The twisting avenues of the web could not be trusted except to tempt the faithful at every turn. Of course, computers could also be used to play computer games, many of which portrayed (or even celebrated) violence. These were definitely nothing a godly family wanted its children experiencing, even in the virtual realm.

As noted, then, computers had no place in the small private school associated with my church. If a family in the congregation had school-age children, it was strongly suggested that its children attend the church's private school. While some families chose to send their children to public school, those families were frowned upon and, like television-owning families, became the subject of harsh gossip.

INTO A SINFUL WORLD

When my parents divorced in the summer after my fifth-grade year, my mother moved with my brother and me, far away from the reaches of our Pentecostal church. While my mother remained a faithful Christian, she could no longer tolerate the severity and rigor our old denomination required. Breaking with the church (to say nothing of moving) meant breaking from its private school. My mother enrolled us in the local public school system. She did this early in the summer, and as the summer waned I grew increasingly anxious about having to attend a "worldly" public school. I worried that I would not fit in, that the other students would regard me as a foreigner, that no one would understand my shyness and resistance to wearing blue jeans, putting on makeup, and watching cartoons.

Thankfully, my childhood sensibilities were still elastic, and I adapted to my surroundings. I overcame the shock of seeing girls wearing pants and makeup and a television in every classroom and hearing curse words pouring from the mouths of almost every student as though their use was an occasion for pride. After a week, I felt that I could settle into a comfortable routine at the school; that is until one embarrassing day in the computer lab.

During the second week of sixth grade, my Social Studies teacher marched a class into the only computer lab on the sixth-grade hallway. Our assignment for that day was to open Word and type up a small project she had given us the night before. I took my seat in front of the black screen and stared at the contraption in front of me. I had never seen such a machine in my entire eleven years! A flush crept up my cheeks as I realized I would have to ask someone how to turn the thing on and use it.

While the computers of the students around me whirred to life, my classmates chatted quietly. As the room settled into a quiet hum of work, I fidgeted in my seat and wondered what I should do. Finally, I leaned toward the girl seated next to me and whispered, "How do I turn it on?"

Her eyebrows rose to the top of her forehead. "You press the power button, dummy," she said before turning back to her own work.

But I still didn't know what to do. I agonized over whether or not to bother the girl again. Finally, I tapped her shoulder and asked, "What does the power button look like?"

She sighed and reached over me to press a large gray button on the bottom of the computer. Exhaling loudly, she drew back toward her own computer.

I smiled my thanks at her. She rolled her eyes. (We never made friends that school year.) Once the computer came to life, I still didn't know what to do. I mashed some buttons and moved the small device attached to the computer around, but it didn't accomplish anything.

The end of the period came quickly. I had never gotten past the opening screen. When my teacher asked me why I didn't have an assignment for submission, I flushed with embarrassment and shrugged my shoulders. In that moment, I was sure she had labeled me, normally a straight-A student, as a lazy degenerate. The bottom line was that I didn't know how to operate the computer, and I couldn't type. Tasked with my simple assignment, I had no idea how to use technology to create the final product. With shame, I accepted the very first zero I had ever received in my young life.

Eventually, my teachers realized I knew nothing about

computers. The school provided me with a peer tutor who kindly walked me through basic functions. Over time, I learned that I could teach myself how to operate many programs on my own by just manipulating them. Still, no matter what I did, I was slower on the computer than my classmates. This slowness in mastering new technologies has never gone away. As a teacher and now as a returning student in a graduate program, I still struggle with my feelings of frustration at this slowness.

LEARNING FROM RELATED EXPERIENCES

While I was struggling to learn a new computer program for my current teaching position, I wondered if any of my fellow students at the Pentecostal private school had had similar experiences. I got back in touch with as many former classmates as I could and was able to conduct several interviews. Out of respect to those individuals who spoke with me, I have changed their names; in addition I withhold the name of the church because many whom I interviewed are still members of the congregation.

"Gareth" is still a member of the church, and he will enroll his daughter in the church's kindergarten program in the fall of 2010. He said he is untroubled by the church's refusal to allow students to use computers: "I'm not that worried about it. Granted, I had to struggle a little bit when I went off to college to learn some of the computer programs, but learning to use a computer wasn't something that I found impossible." He continued, "I completed K–12 at the church's school, and I made it through college and got a decent job. I'm not saying that it wasn't a struggle sometimes, but I'm not willing to allow my child to have access to some of the filth available on the Internet today."

Gareth understands the possibility that his daughter might see something he does not approve of, online or off-line, without his knowledge. "I know I can't monitor her every minute. However, by not having her exposed to [access to computers], it greatly lessens the chance of worldly influence. And when she does need to learn to use a computer, hopefully she will be older and mature enough to make Godly decisions."

"Shauna," also still a member of the church, was more critical of the school's stance toward technology: "As a college student, I constantly have to use the computer to write papers and to create presentations. I felt like an absolute idiot going to my roommate my freshman year and asking her, 'Hey, how do I open a Word document?'" I couldn't help but nod my head in agreement as she continued, "I don't understand why the school still refuses to update their ideas about computers. If a child is going to succeed in the business and working world, she needs those skills." While Shauna still attends the church and abides by its other ideals—she dresses church-appropriately, and she does not own a television set—she did not hesitate to share her regret concerning her own education.

"Corey" no longer attends the church but echoed many of Shauna's opinions. "By not giving children and young adults the tools they need to succeed, the church is really just holding these kids back. My opinion is that children need to learn how to use technology when they are young; otherwise, the acquisition period for learning how to adapt to such tasks will quickly pass by." During our discussion, Corey drew on examples of his own struggles with adapting to new technology: "I honestly think that by not being exposed to computers at a young age, I learn more slowly than a person who did use computers as he or she grew up. Do I think it's unfair? Absolutely! Unfortunately, the blame falls not only with the church but with the parents. I would hope that as adults, the parents of these children would see how much this could harm their technological development. I would hope that parents would want their children to have the same opportunities as other kids."

When I contacted the school's current principal—who directed me not to use his name—he detailed the school's reasoning for continuing to deny students access to computers: "The school understands that students are being asked to use technology in the university system and the workforce. But as young people, their minds are still malleable and easily influenced. Once they become responsible adults and strong members of the church, they should be able to better handle such temptation." I asked him if the school had ever considered providing students with a stripped-down computer with no Internet access and only Microsoft Office programs, since if students were expected to succeed in college or the working world, they would need some knowledge of these programs. Surely students could be spared temptation if not faced with the Internet! His reply was shocking: "We have had several parents ask the same question, and my response has always been the same. Even with such pared-down programs, children can utilize the programs to create inappropriate letters and pictures. If a parent wants his or her child to be exposed to such things, then he or she can send the child to a public school where the child will have to constantly face worldly temptation." With that statement, he ended the call with polite coldness.

WARNING FOR PARENTS

Of course, individuals have the absolute right to believe as they wish; however, in our increasingly plugged-in society, what draconian Pentecostal parents and educators must grow to understand is that limiting our children's access to technology—

tools they will inevitably need in order to succeed in secondary education and the working world—limits their potential. While my experiences within one school are representative of only a small percentage of the student population, all students should have the opportunity for success regardless of the size of the school they come from or percentage of the population they occupy.

Kristi DeMeester is currently pursuing her master's in professional writing at Kennesaw State University in Georgia.

FREE INQUIRY

is published bimonthly by the Center for
Inquiry in association with the Council for
Secular Humanism.
For more information or to subscribe, contact:

Council for Secular Humanism
P.O. Box 664
Amherst, NY 14226-0664 USA

716-636-7571 • www.secularhumanism.org